Understanding DOMINION

Divine Strategies on Living above the World's System and Enjoy the days of Heaven on Earth

CHARLES OMOLE

Copyright ©2010 Charles Omole

Published by: Winning Faith Outreach Ministries
ISBN: 978-1-907095-01-6

London. New York. Boston. Lagos
Published in the United Kingdom.

All Scripture, unless otherwise stated, are taken from the
New King James Version of the Bible. Copyright 1979, 1980, 1982,
1990, Thomas Nelson Inc.

All rights reserved under international Copyright law. This Book is a
seed into the Kingdom of God. Hence contents may be reproduced in
whole or in part in any form for non profit use, without the written
consent of the Author, as long as the Author is credited and such
actions are guarded by integrity and honour.

DEDICATION

This book is dedicated to all the children of God, who are yielded tools in the hand of God; sent to pray, preach & proclaim His Word until Revival comes.

INTRODUCTION

It was on the last day of December 2008 and I was in Kansas City, in the USA. I had just returned to my hotel room preparing for the late night meeting that day in my host Church. I felt prompted to switch on the TV and as I did, I met the tail end of a current affairs programme on the collapsing global financial institutions. What caught my attention was a simple fact that was noted on the programme. That was the fact that more that 75% of the senior management of these collapsing institutions have attended an Ivy League university.

Immediately it came to me that these "smart" and well-educated people are responsible for the collapse of the world's financial system and therefore caused the worst recession in a generation. I, like many people, have always assumed that these smart people really understood what they were doing. Apparently not. Then the Lord spoke to me saying *"I will yet use the foolish things of this world to confound the wise. The wisdom of this world will come to nothing and only the wisdom, which I will give, can bring order to a fallen system. I want you to tell my people that I have already made the provision that will ensure they have full immunity from the perils and limitations of the world's system"*. This encounter birthed the hunger and subsequent work that fashioned this book. In the end, it will take guided "Saints" to put right the huge mess these ungodly "Smart" people have created. No wonder the Bible says that favour is not for the skilful.

The world economies are in recession, but we know that there is no recession in the kingdom of God. So how can believers live above the limitations imposed by this world's system? How can we live in Dominion as God originally instructed in Genesis 1:26-28? In the beginning, God created the heavens and the earth; but what for? Why did God create the earth? Also, the bible tells us that our citizenship is in heaven. If this is true, then we must be on earth as diplomats and ambassadors of heaven.

This FACT grants us Diplomatic Immunity from the limitations of earthly laws and practices; just like any diplomat enjoys immunity in his country of assignment. On earth, a diplomat is not subject to the laws of his/her host country. They are technically above local laws.

On earth, diplomatic immunity is a principle of international law by which certain foreign government officials are not subject to the jurisdiction of local courts and other authorities. The concept of immunity began with ancient tribes. In order to exchange information, messengers were allowed to travel from tribe to tribe without fear of harm. They were protected even when they brought bad news.

Today, immunity protects the channels of diplomatic communication by exempting diplomats from local jurisdiction so that they can perform their duties with freedom, independence, and security. Diplomatic immunity is not meant to **benefit individuals personally per se; it is meant to ensure that foreign officials can do their jobs.** We have been given assignments by God on earth; nothing on it should be able to stop us from fulfilling our assignment. We are supposed to live above earthly limitations.

Understanding Dominion is a book that will answer these questions and reveal God's sovereign provision for world domination by His saints. We are in the world, but not of the world. We are far from oppression. In a time of famine do you have to cut back and make do with less like everybody else? While the world may say yes; the Word says No! The Bible tells us that even in times of famine you can still enjoy the blessing and provision of God.

Jesus said, "*Many widows were in Israel in the days of Elijah, when the heaven was shut up three years and six months, and there was a great famine throughout all the land; but to none of them was Elijah sent except to Zarephath, in the region of Sidon, to a woman who was a widow.*" Luke 4:25

Even though this woman did not have much, she still put God first. And God blessed her for that. He provided for her and her son during the entire famine, keeping them alive when humanly speaking it was impossible. Your survival in a time of famine is not dependent on geography, on economic recovery, on a bailout package, on your ingenuity and skill, but on the faithful promises of God and your obedience to the principles of His Word.

The Word of God says in Philippians 4:19, "*My God shall supply all your need according to His riches in glory by Christ Jesus.*" Notice the supply available to you — it is according to God's resources — not according to the standards set by this world. There is no lack with God; Immunity from Babylon is therefore about how to live on earth with heaven's resources and assets.

This requires that there be interactions between heaven and earth. In this book, I begin by exploring why God created the heavens and the earth. I then go on to explain that as citizens of heaven; we need permanent communication links with the home-country, so that we can live above the systems and restrictions of the earth.

By design; God has put a lot of what we need on our diplomatic mission out of the reach of the enemy on earth. So we need to access heaven from earth to live a life of immunity and dominion. This book is indeed ground breaking in its emphasis that heaven is a place we can access while still alive on earth. A diplomat that is cut-off from his home country is no longer fit to represent it.

I will admonish you to please read the entire book to get the full picture and I can guarantee you that your life will be transformed by its content. Dominion in life is your portion and you will receive fresh insight on how to walk in the grace that commands resources.

I finish the book by explaining how to open a bank account in heaven. This way you can make a withdrawal from heaven's account when the earthly one is empty. You will become unstoppable. So be excited and get ready for spiritual revolution and prosperity revival. Rejoice for increase is here.

May God's best and richest be yours.

Charles Omole
London
2010

TABLE OF CONTENT

Dedication	3
Introduction	5

CHAPTER 1: 13
TOUCHING HEAVEN CHANGING EARTH

CHAPTER 2: 39
LIVING & WINNING BY RIGHTEOUSNESS

CHAPTER 3: 65
INTERACTIONS BETWEEN HEAVEN AND EARTH

CHAPTER 4: 97
A FORETASTE OF HEAVEN

CHAPTER 5: 113
EATING OF THE TREE OF LIFE

CHAPTER 6: 137
ENTERING INTO GOD'S REST

CHAPTER 7: 157
OUR SUFFICIENCY IN HEAVEN

THE EPILOGUE 191

TOUCHING HEAVEN CHANGING EARTH

Thus says the Lord: Learn not the way of the [heathen] nations and be not dismayed at the signs of the heavens, though they are dismayed at them, For the customs and ordinances of the peoples are false, empty, and futile; it is but a tree which one cuts out of the forest [to make for himself a god], the work of the hands of the craftsman with the ax or other tool. They deck [the idol] with silver and with gold; they fasten it with nails and with hammers so it will not fall apart or move around".
Jeremiah 10:2-4 (AMP)

*"Listen to the message that God is sending your way house of Israel. Listen most carefully; **don't take the godless nations as your models.** Don't be impressed by their glamour and glitz no matter how much they are impressed. The religion of this people is nothing but smoke. An idol is nothing but a tree chopped down, then shaped by a woodman's axe. They trim it with a tinsel and balls, use*

hammer and nails to keep it upright. It's like a scarecrow in a cabbage patch; it can't talk, dead wood that has to be carried - can't walk. **Don't be impressed by such stuff it is useless for either good or evil"** **Message version,** God says don't take the Godless nations as your models. One of the challenges and difficulties in the church today is that we have brought what I call the world's models into the church. The world's marketing techniques, seeker sensitive services and so on. The bible says don't take on their models, because we will begin to see that those who have the human knowledge in trouble; like the "experts" managing the collapsing financial institutions in our economies. The Bible says don't take them as your models.

Remember that the wise men saw the Star of Jesus when they were busy focusing on heaven, looking at all the celestial stars. It is foolishness to think that the only way to get latest information is by the Internet and worldly media. Looking unto heaven will give you access to such profound and new information that even the powerful will fear what you carry. As children and ambassadors of God, we need to learn to connect with home-base and not focus too much on the land of our assignment for instructions and guidance.

"Or else, if you will not let My people go, behold, I will send swarms of flies on you and your servants, on your people and into your houses. The houses of the Egyptians shall be full of swarms of flies, and also the ground on which they stand. 22 And in that day I will set apart the land of Goshen, in which My people dwell, that no swarms of flies shall be there, in order that you may know that I am the LORD in the midst of the land. 23 I will make a difference between My people and your people. Tomorrow this sign shall be".
Exodus 8:21-23

The land of Goshen is part of the geographical land of Egypt. Even the swarms knew where not to go. Think about it, they did not just fly where they liked. They knew some areas were not to be visited. We need to understand that there are different and deeper dimensions of God we need to know. The bible says there is a time and season for everything; winter, summer etc. We have to however understand that this does not restrict God, as all the seasons can come together into one, if God wants it to. He is sovereign. We need to understand that when God is in operation all the seasons are suspended easily so don't get yourself entangled by limiting yourself to the natural dimension of things. When God shows up He takes over.

It's important to understand that when we live the days of Heaven on earth then the laws of earth will be subject to the happenings in Heaven. To understand this let's go back to the beginning; Genesis 1:1. *"In the beginning God created the Heavens and the earth"*. In the beginning God created the Heaven and the earth; now I will like to ask a number of questions:

1. "In the beginning God created the Heavens and the earth"; where was God before Heaven was created? This is a question I intend to expand on throughout this book. Right now when you ask people where is God, they say God is in Heaven, but was He homeless before he created Heaven. Genesis 1:1 says "in the beginning...." where was God before Heaven was created? We will see later that God is not in heaven, but rather that heaven is in God. If this confuses your natural mind, then get ready to

increase your capacity to handle and retain Truth from God. Jehovah far exceeds anything our little human mind can capture on its own.

2. When God created Heaven and Earth in Genesis 1:1, did He create one to be inferior to the other? We know that He created the heavens and the earth but why? Because He wanted two places where He could have fellowship. A place to Fellowship comfortably in Heaven and also comfortably on the earth. As we saw in the Garden of Eden, the bible says God would come in and fellowship with Adam. That was the whole idea.

3. If God created the Heavens and the earth in such a way that one is not inferior to the other and He created both of them so that He could have fellowship in both, should the standard of living in one be different from the other? For example, the Queen of England; she has Buckingham Palace in London and several other palaces around

the country. If you look at Buckingham palace and examine the interior decoration standard; and then look at the other Palaces, you will find that they are of equal standard. She does not live in the servant-quarters' in Windsor County and then have a big palace in London. All her palaces reflect the level of her wealth and authority. The President of America lives in the White House, but he has a retreat called Camp David. Camp David is not a one bedroom ghetto apartment, while the white house is big and prestigious. Because of who he is, the standard of living in one place is no different from the other.

So if God created the Heavens and the earth and one is not inferior to the other; then the standard of living in one should not be vastly different from the other, because When God is fellowshipping, He expects the same standard of existence regardless of where He is.

Recently, I read in the media that as a couple were getting divorced; the wife was asking for a lot of money. Her argument was how could the children visit their father in a big house and yet return to live with her in a small basement apartment. Their standard of living must be of comparable standard regardless of which parent they are staying with at any time. Being the legitimate children of their wealthy father, they needed to maintain the same standard of living explained the mother. In the same way, since God created heaven and earth so that He could have fellowship in both places and we don't doubt the standard in Heaven; the question is when He comes to earth is He supposed to behave differently because this is a poor cousin of Heaven? ... no, he is supposed to have the comparable standard. What bothers me is that "if the streets of Heaven are paved with Gold" as many believes literally; how then are we supposed to live here on earth without Gold? If God is supposed to have fellowship both in Heaven and on earth, then there has to be interactions/exchanges between heaven and earth.

We have reduced Heaven to *"my mansion will be bigger than yours"* even though this is not what Heaven is about. Christ is our advocate, He is not in Heaven right now in charge of a construction project. We use scriptures that say, "where I am you will be also", "I am on my way to the Father", "In my Father's house there are many mansions, if it were not so I would have told you so" when Jesus said that He was not on His way to Heaven, He was on His way to the cross. The important lesson here is God created the Heavens and the Earth. How did He create heaven and earth? By His spoken words.

> *Whatever you are experiencing, or whatever you have here on earth that is not a physical model of what exists in Heaven is not supposed to be your portion*

"by the word of the Lord the Heavens were made and all the host of them by the breadth of His mouth, He gathers the waters of the sea together as a heap He lays up the deep in storehouses, let all the earth fear the Lord, let all the inhabitants of the world stand in awe of Him, for He spoke and it was done He commanded and it stood fast". Hallelujah. **In Psalm 33 verse 6-9,** *"Of old you laid the foundations of the earth and the Heavens are the work of your* hand". Psalm 102, Verse 25:

It's important for you to understand that neither is inferior to the other; both are God's handiwork. If God created both heaven and earth, one cannot be a poor cousin of the other. Hallelujah. To help you understand this as we go deeper into this discuss, I will show you some interactions between heaven and earth for you to begin to see that both places have God's DNA in them. Heaven is a place, Heaven is also an experience. But we know that in a court of law, you are not allowed to testify about an event or something you are not a witness to.

Ask yourself as you go round talking to people about Heaven; have you seen Heaven? What interactions have you had with heaven? How authoritative are you in sharing with other people that there is Heaven when you yourself don't know what or where it is? This is the fundamental of why our witnessing is not as impacting as it should be. Because we are testifying about a place we don't even know much about. So if in a natural court of law, hearsay evidence is not admissible then why would it be admissible in the court of the Spirit? That is why spiritually speaking, you need to be an eyewitness to give effective evidence of what you have witnessed; which is why the bible says we can have the days of heaven here on earth. When we look at some of the interactions between heaven and earth in the coming chapters; this thesis will become clearer. In the Bible, we see that people spoke on earth and God heard in Heaven and God spoke in Heaven and people heard on earth. The question is "where is Heaven"? It's important for you to understand that Heaven is a place but is also an experience. The same with hell, you can be in hell before you get to Hell. You need to understand that if you have not had an experience of heaven on earth, you cannot be an effective witness of heaven on earth. Hallelujah.

THE SPIRITUAL CONTROL THE PHYSICAL

The standard of living of God's family in Heaven and earth should never be different. We are on earth as heaven's ambassadors. Everything that truly exists in the natural should be a physical manifestation of what already exists in the spirit if it is to last. The bible says "thy will be done on earth as it is in heaven". In other words, what is happening on earth is already happened in Heaven. For instance, the bible talks about the Ark of God in Heaven, the temple and tabernacle of God in Heaven, even earthquakes in Heaven; nothing happens here on earth that does not have its existence rooted in the Spirit. Whatever you are experiencing, or whatever you have here on earth that is not a physical model of what exists in Heaven is not supposed to be your portion. So if they say you have cancer; is there cancer in Heaven? If the answer is no, then it means you are not supposed to have it. The Bible says whatever can be seen is temporary and subject to change, but whatever cannot be seen is eternal. This means if the entire basis for the existence of something is earthly with no root in the spirit; then it is temporary and subject to change. But if it is a physical manifestation of a spiritual (unseen) reality; then it is eternal and yours for keeps. It means the cancer does not have a spiritual root of existence. Its root is limited to the earth.

Hence you can stand and declare that cancer should go because it does not exist where it matters. It will have no choice but disappear. Also, that is why *"the blessing of the Lord maketh rich and it adds no sorrow to it"*, because the root of the blessing is in Heaven. The bible also talks about "laying treasures for yourself in Heaven" so that whatever happens on earth, depression, inflation or famine, does not affect you financially because your source is in Heaven and as long as the root source is not changing then your physical experience should not change. But whatever you have physically that is not a reproduction of what exists in Heaven then you can get rid of it.

Living a life of dominion means living here on earth based on the experiences, the privileges and the resources in Heaven. **Understanding this will make you earth-proof in your experiences.** Whatever does not exist in Heaven should not exist in you right now. It means before you get to Heaven (the Place), you are already experiencing it. Praise God.

"And it shall come to pass that if ye shall hearken diligently unto my commandments which I command you this day, to love the Lord your God, and to serve him with all your heart and with all your soul; then I will give you the rain for your land in its season, the first rain and the latter rain, that thou mayest gather in thy corn, and thy wine and thine oil. And I will send grass in your fields for your livestock that you

*may eat and be filled. Take heed to yourself lest your heart be deceived and you turn aside and serve other gods and worship them, lest the Lord's anger be aroused against you and He shut up the Heavens so there will be no rain and the land yield not her products and you perish quickly from the good land which the Lord has given you. Therefore shall ye lay up these my words of mine in your heart and in your soul, and bind them as a sign upon your hand that they may be as frontlets between your eyes. You shall teach them to your children speaking of them when you sit in your house, when you walk by the way, when you lie down and when you rise up and you shall write them on the doors of the post of your house and on your gates, that **your days and days of your children may be multiplied in the land which the Lord swore to your fathers to give them as the days of Heaven upon the earth".*** Deuteronomy 11:13-21.

This scripture talks about the <u>longevity</u> and <u>quality</u> of our earthly experience; being comparable to that in heaven. In other words you live here on earth with the resources of Heaven, above the earthly system, as citizens of Heaven. The Bible says we are a stranger in a strange land; in other words we are not supposed to conform to the ways of the world and that is why the

Bible says *"even though we are in the world, we are not of the world"*.

"I am a stranger and a temporary resident on the earth; hide not Your commandments from me." Psalm 119:19

We as believers, are not supposed to live according to their standards in the world; don't copy them; don't model yourselves after the heathen cities because we are supposed to live in dominion on earth. Our experience is supposed to be different. What was said in verse 21 of Deuteronomy 11 was repeated in psalm 89, because we need more than one witness. From verse 11 of psalm 89 the bible says *"the Heavens are yours and the earth also is yours; as for the world and the fullness thereof thou has founded them"*.

Verse 24 *"But my faithfulness and my mercy shall be with him and in my name his horn shall be exalted"*. *Also I will set his hand over the sea and his right hand over the rivers he shall cry to me you are my father, my God and the rock of my salvation. Also I will make him my firstborn, higher than the kings of the earth. My mercy will I keep for him for evermore and my covenant shall stand fast with him"*.

Verse 29, "*His seed also will I make to endure forever and his throne as the days of Heaven*".

God has his families both in Heaven and on earth so both places have to be able to reflect a standard worthy of God's reputation.

Ephesians 2 verses 19-21 "*now therefore you are no longer strangers and foreigners, but fellow citizens with the saints and **members of the household of God**: having been built upon the foundation of the apostles and prophets. Jesus Christ himself being the chief corner stone*"; *in whom the whole building being fitted together grow into a holy temple in the Lord, in whom ye also are builded together for an habitation of God through the Spirit.*

Ephesians 3:14; "*for this reason I bow my knees to the father of our Lord Jesus Christ, from whom **the whole family in Heaven and earth** is named*". So God has families in both places. From verse 16; "*He will grant you according to the riches of His glory to be strengthened with might by His Spirit in the inner man; that Christ may dwell in your hearts by faith; that ye, being rooted and grounded in love may be able to comprehend with all saints what is the breadth, and length and depth and height, and to* *know the love of Christ which passeth knowledge that ye might be filled with all the fullness of God"*

So you have to understand that you have connections to both Heaven and earth whilst still living. You are not just an earthly being or purely just a Heavenly being otherwise you would not have a physical body. So you are supposed to be connecting with Heaven while you are here on earth.

First Corinthians Chapter 15 verse 49: *"As we are born the image of the earthly man so shall also be that we shall also bear the image of the Heavenly man"* the new living translation of First Corinthians Chapter 15 verse 49 says *"just as we are now like the earthly man we will some day be like the Heavenly man"*. As it is in Heaven so it is on earth. Hallelujah.

"Then the temple of God was opened in heaven, and the ark of His covenant was seen in His temple. And there were lightnings, noises, thunderings, an earthquake, and great hail". Revelations 11:19

These things exists here on earth because it also exists in Heaven.

Rev. 15:5, *"after these things I looked and behold the temple of the tabernacle of the testimony in Heaven was opened; and the seven angels came out of the temple, having the seven plagues clothed in pure and white linen and having their breasts girded with golden girdles. And one of the four beasts gave unto the seven angels seven golden vials full of the wrath of God, who liveth forever and ever. And the **temple was filled with smoke from the glory of God and from His power;** and **no man was able to enter into the temple**, till the seven plagues of the seven angels were fulfilled"*.

When everything was done and the temple was ready it was filled with

> *God has his families both in Heaven and on earth so both places have to be able to reflect a standard worthy of God's reputation.*

smoke representing the glory of the Lord. And the bible says no man was able to enter. But also on earth; that is the same thing that happened, if you look at Exodus Chapter 40, when the tabernacle was completed. Verse 34 says **"then a cloud covered the tent of the congregation, and the glory of the Lord** *filled the tabernacle and Moses was not able to enter the tabernacle because the cloud abode thereon and the glory of the Lord filled the tabernacle".* As it is in Heaven so it is on earth.

When a permanent temple was later erected to God in Jerusalem listen to what happened. When this new completed temple had the Ark of God moved into it. First King Chapter 8 verse 10-11 *"and it came to pass when the priests were come out of the holy place, that the cloud filled the house of the Lord. So that the priests could not stand to minister because of the cloud; for the glory of the Lord had filled the house of the Lord".* As it is in Heaven so it is on earth. God wants to feel at home both in Heaven and on earth – that's why the earth is modelling the things in Heaven, so that God can just show up and feel at home.

There are some stores like Costco, IKEA etc that are all over the world. They endeavour to arrange their stores in the same way. In such a way that it does not matter which branch you visit, you don't spend long time trying to find out where items are, as you immediately know where to go because they have designed it identically to the local store you visit regularly. God wants to just show up on earth and feel at home exactly as He feels in Heaven. That is God's agenda.

The question here is this: Where is Heaven? How do you become a witness of it? What does it mean to be in Heaven? Lots of Christians say things like "when we get to Heaven..." and I am wondering to myself that if we are supposed to live the days of Heaven on earth; I am not waiting till I get to Heaven I want to live its quality of life while I am still here, in such a way that when I get to Heaven; I will feel at home instantly. If you think about it, people say the streets of heaven are paved with gold. In that case, some people will not be able to walk in heaven. Because you have lived with so much poverty mentality here on earth, that if you are taking it literally that the streets are paved with gold you won't be able to walk on it. The whole idea of Heaven and earth is so that God feels at home on earth the same way He feels at home in Heaven; same with you.

So God is preparing you, that's why He says you can live in dominion here on earth. What stops us from enjoying the days of Heaven here on earth is our ignorance, absolutely its our ignorance.

My prayer is that by the time you finish this book, you will understand that living an average life on earth is not a good representation of Heaven. You need to begin to question yourself if the way you are living is the way you would be living if you were in Heaven. If the answer is no, then you need to understand that it is your right to live the days of Heaven on earth. Your story must change.

"If I have told you earthly things, and ye believe not, how shall ye believe, if I tell you of heavenly things? And no man hath ascended up to heaven, but he that came down from heaven, even the Son of man which is in heaven". John 3:12-13 (KJV)

Who is speaking here? Jesus of course. Where was he when he was speaking? On earth. But He said that the person speaking is the son of man who has come from Heaven and who is in heaven. But we know that He was physically on earth when He was speaking. How do you reconcile this? This is what I mean by living a life of dominion. Jesus was physically here on earth but He knew He was permanently connected to Heaven. And because He was permanently connected to Heaven, He was from Heaven and He is in Heaven. Even though physically, He was here on earth. Why did He say *"Son of man ….. in Heaven"* because *"not my will but your will be done"*. Whatever the father says that's what happens. For you and I what does it mean to be in Heaven? How do we experience it?

You need to understand that even though we are physical human beings we are supposed to be spiritually tuned to the things of the spirit. You need to have your spiritual ears and eyes open so that you begin to see things the way Heaven sees it, so that when you look at things on earth, you will see things completely different from others and people will wonder why? Because you are seeing what others don't see.

"After these things I looked and behold a door was opened in Heaven: and the first voice which I heard was as it were, of a trumpet talking with me which said, come up hither and I will shew thee things which must be hereafter.

Immediately I was in the spirit and behold a throne was set in Heaven, and one sat on the throne, and He that sat was to look upon like a Jasper and a sardine stone and there was a rainbow round about the throne, in sight like unto an emerald". Revelations 4: 1

John was physically on earth when he had this experience, so in other words **being in the spirit is being in Heaven** as you are in a state of connection to heaven from earth. Being in the Spirit is being in Heaven. What happened to John was that he was physically here on earth and he got caught up, just like Paul was caught up in the third Heavens. Living the days of Heaven on earth is you being physically here on earth but being connected to the spirit. This is a requirement for dominion living. It means you can be sitting or standing, but your spirit man connects to Heaven and as a result you download everything God wants to say, you get back to reality and you know you have been to Heaven. That is what it means.
You come back to yourself and you begin to make decisions that others think are stupid, but you have heard from Heaven. You begin to go in the direction people think you should not go because you have

heard from Heaven and ultimately you will be vindicated. **So to step into the spirit is to bring Heaven to earth.** Consequently whatever has not been settled in the spirit cannot be manifested in the natural in an enduring way. So it's important that you understand that stepping into the spirit is what it means to be in Heaven, while on earth. And that is the experience many Christians don't have.

Glimpses of Heaven are not new and there are books that have been written by people that God has taken into the spirit to show different things. I remember, one book written over a decade ago called "Ministry of Angels".

Living the days of Heaven on earth is you being physically here on earth but being connected to the spirit. This is a requirement for dominion living.

The authors said that when they had the angelic encounter; they had a burning question in their mind to ask. And that was "how did the wall of Jericho collapse given how thick the wall was"? Although the children of Israel were so close to the wall yet were not crushed. And they recorded in the book the angel said "we used our hands to pushed the wall down from the top".

When connected to heaven, you will begin to hear things that normally you won't hear. It's like a TV signals and radio waves. They exist but unless you have the equipment you can live as if it does not exist. When we live the days of Heaven on earth, it's about you sharpening your spiritual equipment so that even though you are here, physically and naturally, people are seeing you physically; but you are not just physical anymore. You are already receiving from Heaven; you are downloading from Heaven; that is what it means.

This way you begin to experience natural things supernaturally and supernatural things naturally. But the difficulty is that many of us when we are in difficulty we would have focused on human methods first before we even remember God. Many of us tend to go back to God after all the physical buttons we have pressed have not worked.

Chapter 1: Touching Heaven Changing Earth

There are certain battles you cannot fight in your own strength, it's not possible. You need to know where to go and you need to fine-tune the equipment that tunes up to that frequency so that when everyone will be panicking and you will just be calm and smiling.

Whatever there is on earth that is not a reproduction of Heaven's version is temporal and can be changed. I need you as we end this chapter, to begin to look at your life, everything that exists that is not a replica of Heaven is temporal and is subject to change. So diseases will die and lack will vanish. Your life is about to enter a new level in God. I am excited for you. You are blessed.

Note and Review

LIVING & WINNING BY RIGHTEOUSNESS

The Bible says that if we confess our sins, God is faithful and just to forgive us our sins and cleanse us from all unrighteousness. The bible does not say God will give us a new righteousness. Sin can make you break fellowship with God but it does not stop you being righteous because righteousness of God in Christ Jesus is irreversible. Sin can make you break fellowship just like your son if he does something very bad you may decide not to talk to him for the next two hours, but that does not stop him from being your son. He will still answer to your name.

You may say you don't want to see him today, because you are angry about that particular situation. But if someone were to call him by your name, he will answer because that does not change regardless of the specific wrongdoing. And that is what it means to be the righteousness of God in Christ Jesus; but the difficulties that many children of God have is that they don't understand how strong this principle is.

> *If you doubt your position it will be difficult for you to exercise your authority*

If someone says to you that you may be the son of the king of Saudi, until you are clearly able to ascertain this, there are certain things you can't do. It might raise your hopes but you can't start forcing certain doors to open if you don't have proof that you are a Prince. Before we can discuss fully the interactions between heaven and earth we have to resolve the issue of righteousness otherwise whenever you step out of line and the devil makes you feel that you are no longer the righteousness of God, you will cede your authority. Anyone who feels that way can't exercise authority, so it is important we settle this, so that you understand that it is God's will for you to have certain things.

"Hear O Israel; thou art to pass over Jordan this day, to go in to possess nations greater and mightier than thyself, cities great and fenced up to heaven" Deuteronomy 9:1.

The instruction here is that they are to go and possess nations greater and mightier than themselves. That is the mission of mankind on earth – they are greater and mightier than yourself but they are not greater and mightier than your God. Therefore you going in the power of God can dispossess nations.

This means that you apply for a job on paper which looks like you are not qualified to get; those are nations greater and mightier than yourself. But God says go and dispossess it, looking at physical strength, qualification and experience these people will beat you hands down. But God says go there because once I am with you, your experience suddenly becomes irrelevant after all, they will now be dealing with the Ancient of Days.

It's important you understand what God is about to do and get your confidence back in your pursuit of Godly obedience. Walking hand in hand with Jehovah, you are unstoppable. You need to build your confidence in God and not in yourself. Your God is the Lion of the tribe of Judah, the One who is the ever present help in time of need. Heaven is His throne and the earth His footstool; He is the unchanging changer; the all seeing and all knowing God. If God is for you "who" can be against you? Be bold my friend and go and take the land.

"A people great and tall, the descendants of the Anakim, whom you know, and of whom you heard it said, 'Who can stand before the descendants of Anak?'". Deuteronomy 9:2.

Sometimes I use this verse, when telling people who are starting their own business not to be afraid; it's your job, your commission to go and dispossess nations bigger than yourself, the multinationals, of this world, they are yours for the taking. The bible calls them tall and giants.

"Therefore understand today that the LORD your God is He who goes over before you as a consuming fire. He will destroy them and bring them down before you; so you shall drive them out and destroy them quickly, as the LORD has said to you.[4] "Do not think in your heart, after the LORD your God has cast them out before you, saying, 'Because of my righteousness the LORD has brought me in to possess this land'; but it is because of the wickedness of these nations that the LORD is driving them out from before you. [5] It is not because of your righteousness or the uprightness of your heart that you go in to possess their land, but because of the wickedness of these nations that the LORD your God drives them out from before you, and that He may fulfil the word which the LORD swore to your fathers, to Abraham, Isaac, and Jacob. [6] Therefore understand that the LORD your God is not giving you this

> *Walking hand in hand with Jehovah, you are unstoppable. You need to build your confidence in God and not in yourself.*

good land to possess because of your righteousness, for you are a stiff-necked people. Deuteronomy 9:3-6

God is still giving you these victories, even though you are described as stiff necked. The question is why is He doing it if he considers you as stiff necked. He made it clear it's not because of your righteousness. For us to understand righteousness you need to see certain events in the bible so that you understand the awesomeness of the righteousness I am not talking about.

Jacob and Laban: (Genesis 30 verse 33) *"So shall my righteousness answer for me in time to come, when it shall come for my hire before thy face; everyone that is not speckled and spotted among the goats, and brown among the sheep, that shall be counted stolen with me"*.

He said his righteousness would speak for him in the time to come. So note the word Righteousness here. Again we see the same in the story of **Abimelech**. Genesis Chapter 20 verse 4 *"But Abimelech had not yet come near her: and he said "Lord, wilt thou slay also a righteous nation?"* He said – I did this in the integrity of my heart. The reason for these two examples is because the righteousness referred to in these two verses is what I call **"conformity with moral law"** it is not the righteousness you win by; it is not the righteousness of God in Christ Jesus. When Jacob said my "righteousness" he meant his honesty. This is observance of human law. The question is which righteousness do you live and win by? The righteousness you win by is not what you call honesty or by doing the right thing. Which is the righteousness you win by?

Exodus Chapter 15: 1, 12-13 – the song of Moses.
*Then sang Moses and the children of Israel this song unto the Lord and spake saying: "I will sing unto the Lord for He has triumphed gloriously, the horse and rider hath he thrown into the sea. The Lord is my strength and song, and He is become my salvation he is my God and I will prepare him an inhabitation; my father's God, and I will exalt him. The Lord is a man of war, the Lord is His name". "thou stretchedst out thy right hand, the earth swallowed them". "Thou in thy mercy hast led forth the people which thou has redeemed; thou has guided them in **thy strength** unto thy holy habitation"*

Key point here is you have guided them <u>in Your strength</u>. Not in their own strength, but in Your strength.

Also, 1Sam 2:1,9 the song of Hannah.
"And Hannah prayed and said, my heart rejoiceth in the Lord, mine heart is exalted in the Lord; my mouth is enlarged over mine enemies because I rejoice in thy salvation". *"He will guard the feet of His saints, but the wicked shall be silent in darkness; for **by strength shall no man prevail**"*.

So Moses said God guided them in his strength alone and Hannah also said "for by strength shall no man prevail.

WHAT IS THE RIGHTEOUSNESS YOU CAN WIN BY?

Romans 10 from verse 1: *"Brethren my hearts desire and prayer to God for Israel is that they might be saved. For I bear them record that they have a zeal of God, but not according to knowledge, for they being ignorant, of **God's righteousness**, and seeking to establish **their own righteousness** have not submitted themselves unto the **righteousness of God**"*.

Immediately you can see the Bible has mentioned two types of righteousness. They are following their own righteousness which is observance or following human laws, regulations, or edicts. It is important to understand that operating in the righteousness of God is not observance of human laws.

If you do not understand fully that you are operating in the righteousness of God or you do not understand the ramifications of that statement, it will be difficult for you to live a life of dominion on earth; because you will always be cowed by the deceptions and accusations of the enemy.

Isaiah 51 verse 1: *"Hearken to me ye that **follow after righteousness**, ye that seek the Lord; look unto the rock whence ye are hewn, and to the hole of the pit whence ye are digged. Look to Abraham your fathers and unto Sarah that bare you; for I called him alone, and blessed him, and increased him"*.

Verse 5: *"My righteousness is near; my salvation is gone forth, and mine arms shall judge the people; the isles shall wait upon me, and on mine arm shall they trust"*.

Verse 7: *"Hearken unto me, ye that **know righteousness**, the people whose heart is my law; hear ye not the reproach of men, neither be ye afraid of their reviling"*.

Are you following after righteousness or do you know righteousness? Do you know Him?

THERE ARE 3 TYPES OF RIGHTEOUSNESS:

Righteousness of man which produces filthiness.

"But we are all as an unclean thing, and all our righteousnesses are like filthy rags; Isaiah 64:6.

This is when people want to use their will to do the right thing. There are some people who are not saved but are good people. They observe all the laws of man – this is the righteousness of man which the bible says is as "filthy rags". The righteousness of man on the face of it might seem okay, but God considers it as filthiness. So it is important that you understand that it is not the righteousness by which we operate or win by.

The second type of **righteousness is the righteousness of the law**. Righteousness which produces consciousness of sin.

Romans 3 verse 20. *"Therefore by the deeds of the law there shall no flesh be justified in His sight; for by the law is the knowledge of sin"*.

> *Clearly people are more mature than others but that does not change the fundamental fact that we are all in Christ, equally righteous.*

The third type of righteousness is the **righteousness of faith**. This is the righteousness of God, the righteousness to live by.

*"But now **the righteousness of God without the law is manifested**, being witnessed by the law and the prophets; even the righteousness of God which is by faith of Jesus*

*Christ unto all and upon all them that believe; for there is no difference; for all have sinned and come short of the glory of God. Being justified freely by His grace through the redemption that is in Christ Jesus; whom God hath set forth to be a **propitiation through faith** in His blood, to declare His righteousness for the remission of sins that are past, through the forbearance of God"*. Romans 3:21-25

Every believer has the same righteousness. Assume we have a group of three people who are all male for the purpose of this illustration. Two of them are well known Pastors and the other a new Christian; all three people have the same level of righteousness. **We need to understand that when they are standing to proclaim access to what God has, they all have equal access.** As Christians we have developed a dependency culture whereby we feel we need to talk to a Pastor, who will then talk to God on our behalf. We all have access to God equally.

Clearly people are more mature than others and that maturity brings knowledge that allows you to be able to enjoy the reality of redemption more than another; but that does not change the fundamental fact that we are all in Christ equally righteous. **From this illustration, it is clear that although one person's walk with God might be deeper than another, it does not change the fact that we all have equal access to God from the platform of faith in God.** It is important that you don't think that one person is more righteous than the other; you are as righteous as the man preaching on TV, you are as righteous as that man who wrote that best selling gospel book; every believer has the same righteousness. We can practice righteousness more than each other due to maturity in God and knowledge of Him, but we all have the same righteousness of faith in Christ Jesus.

What you see when people manifest Gods presence more than others is not increase in righteousness, but increase in maturity. It is very important that you understand you are as righteous as that man or woman of God you admire.

OPERATING IN THE RIGHTEOUSNESS OF GOD

Romans 3:19 – 22
Now we know that whatever the law says, it says to those

who are under the law, that every mouth may be stopped, and all the world may become guilty before God. Therefore by the deeds of the law no flesh will be justified in His sight, for by the law is the knowledge of sin. But now the righteousness of God apart from the law is revealed, being witnessed by the Law and the Prophets, even the righteousness of God, through faith in Jesus Christ, to all and on all who believe. For there is no difference;

You need to understand is that, what did not obtain righteousness for you cannot then take it away from you. The righteousness of God is not a temporary activity it is permanent. Did you become the righteousness of God by stopping smoking, not lying, by being honest? Those are not the things that got you righteous, **you got the righteousness by faith in Christ Jesus**.... What did not get you the righteousness cannot take it away from you. When you sin you break fellowship but you are still the righteousness of God in Christ Jesus, because not sinning did not get you there in the first place.

Do not listen to the lie of the devil, whereby he is able to hang a sin over your head like a sword and every time you want to exercise your authority, he brings it to your remembrance. You can tell him to shut up because your not sinning did not obtain you righteousness in the first place.

If as you thought before, when you sin God just cut you off complete; how would He be able to hear you when you confess your sins? He that covers his sins will not prosper, but if we confess our sins He is faithful and just to forgive us all our sins and forgive us all unrighteousness. The question is while we are confessing our sins how is He able to hear if we are not within earshot of Him. If suddenly every time you sin, God exports you somewhere far away on a one way ticket; How will He know you are sorry? When you say you are sorry and God hears you and forgives you, it's on the basis of you being His righteousness has not changed even though you sinned. Yes, fellowship might have been affected, but your being His righteousness is by faith in Christ Jesus and not according to the law. Amen. You need to understand this very carefully and develop boldness for dominion in life. To wrap this up, there are five things you must understand about operating in the righteousness of God.

1. Every time you look at the subject of righteousness one thing should always be on your mind: **"What is at stake is your justification"?** This means it is either we are justified by faith or not at all. So we are righteous for no other reason than that God has declared us righteous. It does not matter what sin you have committed, God has declared you justified.

Romans Chapter 3 verse 20
"Therefore by the deeds of the law there shall no flesh be justified in his sight: for by the law is the knowledge of sin". In other words you are righteous for no other reason than the fact that God has declared you righteous.

And the gifts and calling of God are without repentance. You need to hold on to this. The bible says that *"For the lord has commended his love towards us in that while we were still sinners, He died for us"*. Christ already died for the ungodly. Even the people going around today saying there is no God. God has already died for them. God's relationship with man is not "I love you because you love me". God's relationship with man is "I love you, full stop". Even though man does not yet love God, even though man may be denying the existence of God; God is saying I still love you anyway. If that is the case for people who don't agree God exists, how much more you who have now been sanctified by the blood of the Lamb.

God does not love you because you are a nice man or woman, or because of what you have done, He just loves you. Nothing else matters. It is absolutely important that you understand what justification means. God has declared you justified and it is on this basis that you have become the righteousness of God in Christ Jesus. It is irreversible. It is important therefore that you come to a knowledge that it does not matter what sin you have committed, you can still go boldly to the throne of grace, confess your sins and begin to declare what God wants you to declare. You cannot live in dominion on earth if you are cowed by the fear of sins you have committed in the past. That is the tactic of the enemy.

2. **You cannot earn God's righteousness;** it is His act of grace through Christ Jesus. 2 Cor 5 verse 16 *"From now on, regard no one according to the flesh, yea though we have known Christ after the flesh, yet now*

henceforth know we Him no more. Therefore if anyone is in Christ, he is a new creation, old things have passed away; behold all things are become new. Now all things are of God who hath reconciled us to Himself by Jesus Christ, and hat given to us the ministry of reconciliation. To wit, that God was in Christ, reconciling the world unto himself not imputing their trespasses unto them; and hath committed unto us the word of reconciliation".

You cannot earn God's righteousness it is an act of Grace through Jesus Christ. John 3:16 says *"For God so loved the world that He gave His only begotten son that whosoever believes in Him should not perish but have everlasting life".*

This is a one way traffic in that God commended His love towards us, it cannot be earned. When you realise this you know that you have to begin to deal with things that cut fellowship, but never shirk from the fact that you are the righteousness of God in Christ Jesus. Grace is not simply leniency when we have sinned. Grace is the enabling gift of God not to sin. Grace is power, not just pardon. Therefore the effort we make to obey God is not an effort done in our own strength, but in the strength which God supplies. The duties God requires of us are not in proportion to the strength we possess in ourselves. Rather, they are proportional to the resources available to us in Christ. We do not have the ability in ourselves to accomplish the least of God's tasks. This is a law of grace. When we recognise it is impossible to perform a duty in our own strength, we will discover the secret of its accomplishment

You must not question the fundamentals of whether you are the righteousness of God in Christ Jesus. God who does not waiver gave it to you. Once you accept Christ you are the righteousness of God in Christ Jesus.

3. **If I am the righteousness of God, what happens when I sin?** If and when you sin, **it does nothing to your righteousness**. When we sin we break fellowship, but never break relationship. Your sinlessness did not make you righteousness if you are a born again child of God; so you need to regain your boldness in God.

1 John 1 verse 5-8 *"this is the message which we have heard of Him and declare unto you, that God is light, and in Him is no darkness at all. If we say that we have fellowship with Him, and walk in darkness, we lie, and do not the truth: but if we walk in the light, as He is in the light, we have fellowship with one another and the blood of Jesus Christ His Son cleanseth us from all sin. If we say we have no sin, we deceive ourselves, and the truth is not in us. If we confess our sins, He is faithful and just to forgive us our sins, and to cleanse us from all unrighteousness".*

> Grace is not simply leniency when we have sinned. Grace is the enabling gift of God not to sin.

Verse 8 tells us we will be cleansed from all unrighteousness not that we will be made righteous again. Sin can break fellowship but it does not make you unrighteous after you are already saved.

In Zachariah 3:1-2, talking about the vision of Christ to come, the bible says *"And he shewed me Joshua the high priest standing before the angel of the Lord and satan standing at the right hand to resist him. And the Lord said unto satan, The Lord rebuke thee o Satan; even the Lord that hath chosen Jerusalem rebuke thee is this not a brand plucked from the fire, now Joshua was clothed with filthy garments and was standing before the angel. And He answered and spake unto those that stood before Him, saying, take away the filthy garments from him".*

Isaiah Chapter 61 verse 10: " *I will greatly rejoice in the Lord, my soul shall be joyful in my God: for He hath clothed me with the garments of salvation, he hath covered me with the robe of righteousness, as a bridegroom decketh himself with ornaments, and as a bride adorneth herself with jewels".*

God exchanged our filthy garments for robes of righteousness. When you sin you do not need a new robe, you only need to clean the one you have. When you sin its as if there is a spot on your robe, and you get detergent and clean that dirt away and your robe is okay again. That is what the Blood of Jesus has done for us. It is very important for you to understand this.

4. **Believers do not put on a robe any more, we put on a person and His name is Jesus, he is our**

Righteousness, He is our Redemption and He is our Justification.

1 Corinthians 1:30 states; *"But of Him are ye in Christ Jesus, who of God is made unto us wisdom, and righteousness, and sanctification and redemption"*

Isaiah 51 verse 1: *"Hearken to me ye that **follow after righteousness**, ye that seek the Lord; look unto the rock whence ye are hewn, and to the hole of the pit whence ye are digged. Look to Abraham your fathers and unto Sarah that bare you; for I called him alone, and blessed him, and increased him"*.

Verse 7: *"Hearken unto me, ye that **know righteousness**, the people whose heart is my law; hear ye not the reproach of men, neither be ye afraid of their reviling"*.

Isaiah 51 verse 1 talks of those who follow after righteous while verse 7 talks about those who know righteousness. We now understand that righteousness is a person, i.e. Christ. **All some people do is follow after Christ, they don't really know Him.** And those are the people who try to observe rules and regulations, but once you know righteousness, you know Christ personally and following Him becomes a lot easier. It is important for you to understand that New Testament saints don't put on robes anymore, we put on a person and His name is Jesus. Hence, as He is in heaven so are we on earth.

> *Deception is the number one tool of the enemy. You must therefore understand that he still uses the same trick*

2 Corinthians 5 verse 21 states; *"For He made Him who knew no sin, to become sin for us, that we might become the righteousness of God in Christ Jesus"*

5. **Why was Jesus made sin? Because if Jesus was going to have legal right to access hell He needed to become sin.** Jesus would not have been able to go to hell if he was sinless. That would not follow the law, so our sins were imputed on Him. The wages of sin is death, so He paid the price, the word of God has to be obeyed.

The bible says God put all of that on Jesus and killed Him. That way the word of God is fulfilled that says "the soul that sins must die." But by being resurrected and we now believing in Him, we are now no longer supposed to be paying the price because the price has already been paid. That is why when you sin today you can ask for forgiveness knowing that you will not die, because someone else has already paid the price.

On the way out of hell Christ shut the door against those that are righteous. He alone maintains our righteousness. **You stand in all that God is and all that God has you must not be intimidated any more.** Rise up boldly and understand that you are as righteous as any man of God on the face of this earth. Because Christ does not discriminate, they may be more mature than you but you can develop yourself as well. However the fundamentals are the same.

Righteousness is the ability to stand before God without a sense of shame, guilt or inferiority. We need to know righteousness which is Jesus Christ, we then need to believe in our hearts what He has said and we need to declare with our mouth what the word says about us. That is the only way. Now you will understand why I said it will be difficult to talk about living in dominion on earth, without clearing up this issue of righteousness, otherwise it will be difficult for you to practicalise what we will be looking at in future chapters.

What is rightfully yours is yours by virtue of your righteousness in Christ Jesus. Satan is called the accuser of the brethren because that is all he has. You need to have an answer for Satan and that is that you are the righteousness of God in Christ Jesus. The devil specialises in trying to sell you what you already have. Deception is the number one tool of the enemy. You must therefore understand that he still uses the same trick today. In future chapters I will explain what happened after man fell. *"man has become like one of us, knowing good and evil"*. The unity of Trinity that makes 3 to become one indistinguishable; of which man became part by being created in the image of God, was lost when man fell and man now became like "one" of us, not "one of us". The question is "which one"?

Note and Review

INTERACTIONS BETWEEN HEAVEN AND EARTH

The Bible says "thanks be to God in whom all the families in Heaven and earth is named". In other words, there are families in Heaven and there are families on earth and the bible says in First Corinthians 15, *"as we are born the image of the earthly men we shall also bear the image of the Heavenly man.*

We know that heaven is a place and those in Christ will get there someday, but heaven is also an experience. If we are going to have dominion on earth and we know that heaven is a place, the only way we are going to have it is if we have connections between us here on earth and heaven. That way we can begin to bring the days of heaven on earth in terms of our individual experiences.

In the preceding chapter, we looked at the subject of righteousness. I explained that it is not possible to understand fully your power or resources available if you do not fully understand that you are the righteousness of God in Christ Jesus. We looked at it from the perspective of what the righteousness of God is not. We looked at three types of righteousness; the righteousness of the law, the righteousness of man the bible says is like filthy rag and thirdly the righteousness by faith, which is the righteousness of God in Christ Jesus. I also explained that if you are looking at righteousness, we are more or less looking at our justification. And I explained that if we are born again child of God and commit sin the sin does not make you less righteousness, what it does is to break fellowship. I was trying to make you understand that sinning does not make you less righteousness. Clearly we are more mature than others, and our ability to walk in the reality of our redemption will vary based on that maturity.

John Chapter 3 verse 12 says (these words were spoken deliberately for our edification) *"If I have told you earthly things, and ye believe not, how shall ye believe, if I tell you of heavenly things?"*

In other words you are programmed largely to deal with earthly things, but because I want you to experience heavenly things while you are still here on earth, you are supposed to be re-programming your mind while you are here on earth to deal with heavenly things.

WHERE IS HEAVEN?

Verse 13: ***"And no man hath ascended up to heaven, but he that came down from heaven even the Son of man which is in heaven"***. How does this make sense? We know where Jesus was when he was speaking, He was on earth, and we know he was referring to himself. So He was physically here on earth when making that assertion. He is confirming that although physically on earth; He was also in heaven by interaction. He was enjoying interaction between heaven and earth; living on earth based on heaven,s command, standards and principles.

Jesus was saying; "Whatever I hear God say is what I say". It's important that you understand what it means to live the days of heaven on earth. It does not mean dying and going to heaven; it's living a length and quality of life that reflects heavens standards. Whatever is not in heaven if it exists here on earth it is temporary; it's something you can get rid of i.e., disease and sickness. If it does not exist in heaven, then its root is very shallow.

> *Nothing on earth ever comes as a surprise to you because God does not begin what he has not already finished.*

Revelations 4 verse 1 says *"After this I looked and behold a door was opened in heaven";* Where was John when this happened? He was on earth. Doesn't that surprise you? How can someone here on earth be able to see what is happening in heaven. This demonstrates the connections between heaven and earth. Apostle John went further; *"And the first voice I heard was like a trumpet which said come up hither, and I will shew thee things which must be hereafter".*

That's one of the benefits of living the days of heaven on earth. Nothing on earth ever comes as a surprise to you because God does not begin what he has not already finished. As a result you are able to eavesdrop on conversations in heaven. You are able to see what is going to happen hereafter.

So, while everyone is running like headless chickens everywhere, you are just standing still where you are, because you know what you have received from heaven. therefore you are not following the crowd. Lots of people tend to follow the crowd because they have no direction, and sadly people of God do the same.

For example, the day Jacob made that deal with Laban in Genesis Chapter 30, the only reason Laban agreed to that deal was because he felt since most of his animals are not spotted; Jacob would stand no chance of success. So as far as Laban was concerned; he was getting a good deal. If on that day you had been asked to come and invest in Jacob plc how many of you would agree? The facts say that investing in Jacob plc would lose you money. Whereas investing in Laban plc ... looked good on paper. But through connections between heaven and earth, you can eavesdrop on heaven's conversation and download the details into your spirit. This new revelation will then informed your choices on earth. We saw later in the Bible that the wealth of Laban was transferred to Jacob. Jacob used heaven's technology to convert all Laban's stock to spotted animals.

If at the end you are then asked to invest in Jacob plc, you now quickly do so. Why? Because you can now see the result; this is what tend to happen, rather than following the lead of the spirit and do things even when they seem not to make natural sense. This is what the interaction between heaven and earth does to you. It allows you to begin to make guided decisions; (when others think it doesn't make sense), not because you are crazy, not because you are following the crowd, but because you are following the leading of the spirit. This is the beauty of divine guidance.

"After these things I looked, and behold, a door standing open in heaven. And the first voice which I heard was like a trumpet speaking with me, saying, "Come up here, and I will show you things which must take place after this." **Immediately I was in the Spirit; and behold, a throne set in heaven,** *and One sat on the throne. And He who sat there was like a jasper and a sardius stone in appearance; and there was a rainbow around the throne, in appearance like an emerald. Around the throne were twenty-four thrones, and on the thrones I saw twenty-four elders sitting, clothed in white robes; and they had crowns[b] of gold on their heads. And from the throne proceeded lightnings, thunderings, and voices. Seven lamps of fire were burning before the throne, which are the[d] seven Spirits of God".* Rev. 4:1-5

"Immediately I was in the spirit; and behold a throne was set in heaven". This means he was in the spirit and then he began to explain what he was actually seeing and interacting with in heaven; but we also know that he was not dead during this experience. Hence, he was interacting with heaven from the earth. You must be permanently hooked to the source. To make this very clear to you; I want us to look at some of the examples of basic interactions between heaven and earth. We will be exploring this over the next few chapters.

FOOD

The first example of interaction between heaven and earth is food.

"Then the **LORD** **appeared** *to him by the terebinth trees of Mamre, as he was sitting in the tent door in the heat of the day. So he lifted his eyes and looked, and behold, three men were standing by him; and when he saw them, he ran from the tent door to meet them, and* **bowed himself to the ground,** *and said, "My Lord, if I have now found favour in Your sight, do not pass on by Your servant. Please let a little water be brought, and wash your feet, and rest yourselves under the tree. And I will bring a morsel of bread, that you may refresh your hearts. After that you may pass by, inasmuch as you have come to your servant. They said, "Do as you have said."* Genesis 18:1-5

[9]*And they said to him, Where is Sarah your wife? And he said, [She is here] in the tent.* [10]***[The Lord] said, I will surely return to you when the season comes round, and behold, Sarah your wife will have a son.*** *And Sarah was listening and heard it at the tent door which was behind Him.* Genesis 18:9-10 (AMP)

Does God eat? From the above scripture, we can see that this is the Lord manifesting in bodily form. If you are familiar with the scriptures, you will know that those three men could not have been angels. Throughout the scriptures every time man tried to bow down to worship angels, they have been corrected and told not to do so because Angels understood their position.

"And I, John, am he who heard and witnessed these things. And when I heard and saw them, I fell prostrate before the feet of the messenger (angel) who showed them to me, to worship him. 9But he said to me, Refrain! [You must not do that!] I am [only] a fellow servant along with yourself and with your brethren the prophets and with those who are mindful of and practice [the truths contained in] the messages of this book. Worship God! Revelation 22:8-9

These were not all just angels in Gen.18. One of the three guests was the Lord, and since God the Father was never seen in bodily form (John 1:18), only the "Angel of the covenant," Christ Himself, can be meant here; see especially Gen. 18:22.

Also if you read the commentary on Gen. 16:7 you will get further enlightenment. "The Angel of the Lord" or "of God," or "of His presence" is readily identified with the Lord God (Gen. 16:11, 13; 22:11, 12; 31:11, 13; Exod. 3:1-6 and other passages). But it is obvious that the "Angel of the Lord" is a distinct person in Himself from God the Father (Gen. 24:7; Exod. 23:20; Zech. 1:12, 13 and other passages). Nor does the "Angel of the Lord" appear again after Christ came in human form. He must of necessity be One of the "three-in-one" Godhead. The "Angel of the Lord" is the visible Lord God of the Old Testament, as Jesus Christ is of the New Testament. Thus His deity is clearly portrayed in the Old Testament. The **Cambridge Bible** observes, *"There is a fascinating forecast of the coming Messiah, breaking through the dimness with amazing consistency, at intervals from Genesis to Malachi. Abraham, Moses, the slave girl Hagar, the impoverished farmer Gideon, even the humble parents of Samson, had seen and talked with Him centuries before the herald angels proclaimed His birth in Bethlehem."*

Gen 18 Verses 4-5 *"Let a little water I pray you, be fetched, and wash your feet, and rest yourselves under the* *tree: And I will fetch a morsel of bread, and comfort ye your hearts; and after that ye shall pass on: inasmuch as you have come to your servant. They said "you may do as you have said". And Abraham hurried into the tent and unto Sarah, and said "Make ready quickly three measures of fine meal, knead it, and make cakes upon the hearth".*

This is a slight digression; but we need to bring lessons out of every scripture as we go along. Sarah could easily have said "you did not give me notice they were coming today" or "it's not on my to-do list today". And that is why husbands and wives need to understand that there are things that can happen spontaneously and not allow dogma to begin to overrule the things of the spirit. If the husband does this every day of the year, bringing people in unannounced, then it becomes a different thing. But when something like this happens, you can see that the wife even though she had other plans for the day, went along without any problem. Lesson for wives there I believe.

Gen.18:7 *"And Abraham ran unto the herd and fetched a calf tender and good, and gave it unto a young man; and he* *hastened to dress it. And he took butter, and milk, and the calf which he had dressed, and set it before them; and he stood by them under the tree, and **they did eat**".*

Who was eating here? Here we see Lord God eating man's food. If this truth challenges your long held tradition; it is supposed to. We all need to increase our capacity to receive and retain deep truth from the Word; if we are to exercise dominion on earth.

Gen. 18 Verse 9 *Then they said to him, "where is Sarah your wife? And he said "behold in the tent. "And he said, I will certainly return unto thee according to the time of life; and lo; Sarah thy wife shall have a son".*

Another question is what food did the children of Israel eat when they were in the wilderness? They ate manna; **so in the wilderness man ate heavenly food.** Accordingly can you see the interactions taking place here? I am trying to show the interactions between heaven and earth.

"Thy will be done on earth as it is in heaven"; this is interaction between heaven and earth. They **ate**

manna from heaven; man ate heaven's food and the Lord God ate man's food and that is an interaction between heaven and earth. **God wants to be able to have fellowship in both places.**

It is important that you understand that the whole idea was for God to be able to feel at home in both places; however that changed with what happened in the garden. What He is now saying is that you on earth and who is in Me can live in dominion on earth; establishing My Kingdom in the process. In other words the earth may not change but your experience will.

SPIRITUAL ELEVATION

*"Now He said to Moses, "**Come up** to the LORD, you and Aaron, Nadab and Abihu, and seventy of the elders of Israel, and worship from afar. 2 And Moses alone shall come near the LORD, but they shall not come near; nor shall the people go up with him."*
3 So Moses came and told the people all the words of the LORD and all the judgments. And all the people answered with one voice and said, "All the words which the LORD has said we will do." 4 And Moses wrote all the words of the

LORD. And he rose early in the morning, and **built an altar at the foot of the mountain, and twelve pillars according to the twelve tribes of Israel.** 5 Then he sent young men of the children of Israel, who offered burnt offerings and sacrificed peace offerings of oxen to the LORD. 6 And Moses took half the blood and put it in basins, and half the blood he sprinkled on the altar. 7 Then he took the Book of the Covenant and read in the hearing of the people. And they said, "All that the LORD has said we will do, and be obedient." 8 And Moses took the blood, sprinkled it on the people, and said, "This is the blood of the covenant which the LORD has made with you according to all these words."

9 Then Moses **went up**, also Aaron, Nadab, and Abihu, and seventy of the elders of Israel, 10 and **they saw the God of Israel**. And there was under His feet as it were a paved work of sapphire stone, and it was like the very heavens in its clarity. 11 But on the nobles of the children of Israel He did not lay His hand. So **they saw God, and they ate and drank**. 12 Then the LORD said to Moses, **"Come up to Me on the mountain** and be there; and I will give you tablets of stone, and the law and commandments which I have written, that you may teach them." **Ex. 24:1-12**

Chapter 3: Interactions between Heaven and Earth

Verses 1 to 9 is about God asking them to **come up and into the Spirit dimension rather than a physical elevation**. What is the evidence of this? If you read verse 12 of Exodus 24, God made a clear distinction *"Then the Lord said to Moses "<u>come up to me into the mount</u> and be there; and I will give thee tables of stone, and a law and commandments which I have written; that thou mayest teach them".*

If in verse 12 He was saying come up to me on the mountains, what "come up" was He saying in the preceding verses 1-9. "Come up" He said, and to make it clear that it's not the same thing, in verse 12 He now told Moses specially **"come up to me on the mountain;"** that is different from **"come up"** in verse one. As a result of the **come up** in verse 1; we see that *"then Moses went up....."*; and **they saw the God of Israel.** *"It was like the heavens in its clarity".* That was a spiritual experience. *They went into the Spirit dimension".* After that experience ended; God now said to Moses alone, *"Come up physically to me into the mountains"* in verse 12.

Remember we are discussing food as an example of interaction between heaven and earth. What food did they eat in Exodus 24; where did they get their drink from? The "up" in verses 1 and 9 is different from the "up" in verse 12. We have seen earlier how the Lord God came down and ate man's food; now living men "went up" and ate God's food. **The Lord came down and ate Abraham's food. The elders went up and ate God's food.** God wants us to have the days of heaven on earth. How can you have such an experience and have sickness in your body. You wake up and God said come up here and you enter heaven in a vision, and you interact with God and you eat there and come down ... whatever the sickness there is in your body, it will flee in terror. Because you no longer have a body it can dwell in.

> *We all need to increase our capacity to receive and retain deep truth from the Word; if we are to exercise dominion on earth.*

What is the food of heaven today? God can still repeat this experience with any of us, as He is sovereign in all things. But that is not what this is about. The certain food of heaven today is "Dabba" – **the proceeding word of God**. "Man shall not live by bread alone, but by every word that proceeds out of the mouth of God".

This is also heavens food which we are supposed to be eating and as we eat the word literally speaking, it enables us to interact with heaven; what you eat determines your strength level. "Dabba" word is also heavenly food we need to eat to gain spiritual strength and stature. "Dabba" word, the proceding word out of the mouth of God. It goes beyond just understanding the bible. "Dabba" relates to Rhema even though Rhema (the revealed Word) will not contradict Logos (the written Word).

It shows you that God wants to feel at home in both places, here we see Moses and the elders having a party in heaven without dying. And that shows what it means when God says He wants you to have the days of heaven on earth. The only way to live in dominion on earth is to begin to interact with heaven.

COMMUNICATION BETWEEN HEAVEN AND EARTH

The second example of interaction between heaven and earth is communication. Can God read? Can God write? Does God speak? Can we hear Him here on earth when He speaks? I would like to show you examples of how man spoke on earth and God heard in heaven and how God spoke in Heaven and man heard on earth. This is to show how communication is one of the key interactions between heaven and earth we need to engage.

The story of Hagar in Genesis 21 gives us more revelation. After they ran out of water, Hagar put Ishmael the lad by a shrub to die and she turned away so that she would not see the lad die, and the lad began to cry and the bible says *"and the Lord heard the cry of the Lad"*.

*"And the water in the skin was used up, and she placed the boy under one of the shrubs. ¹⁶ Then she went and sat down across from him at a distance of about a bowshot; for she said to herself, "Let me not see the death of the boy." So she sat opposite him, and lifted her voice and wept. ¹⁷ **And God heard the voice of the lad.** Then the angel of God called to Hagar out of heaven, and said to her, "What ails you, Hagar? Fear not, **for God has heard the voice of the lad where he is**.*

> We have seen earlier how the Lord God came down and ate man's food; now living men "went up" and ate God's food.

¹⁸ Arise, lift up the lad and hold him with your hand, for I will make him a great nation." ¹⁹ Then God opened her eyes, and she saw a well of water. And she went and filled the skin with water, and gave the lad a drink". Genesis 21:15-19

Where was God? The lad was on earth and God heard the cry in heaven. Before the lad cried, Hagai must have been crying all along. Why was it the cry of the lad that God heard? That is part of the benefit of the Abrahamic covenant. The Lad was still a seed of Abraham and the force of the covenant will compel

God to answer. **The lad cried here on earth and God heard in heaven.**

*"For ask now concerning the days that are past, which were before you, since the day that God created man on the earth, and ask from one end of heaven to the other, whether any great thing like this has happened, or anything like it has been heard. 33 Did any people **ever hear the voice of God speaking out** of the midst of the fire, as you have heard, and live? 34 Or did God ever try to go and take for Himself a nation from the midst of another nation, by trials, by signs, by wonders, by war, by a mighty hand and an outstretched arm, and by great terrors, according to all that the LORD your God did for you in Egypt before your eyes? 35 To you it was shown, that you might know that the LORD Himself is God; there is none other besides Him. 36 **Out of heaven He let you hear His voice, that He might instruct you; on earth He showed you His great fire, and you heard His words** out of the midst of the fire. 37 And because He loved your fathers, therefore He chose their descendants after them; and He brought you out of Egypt with His Presence, with His mighty power, 38 driving out from before you nations greater and mightier than you, to bring you in, to give you their land as an inheritance, as it is this day. 39 Therefore know this day, and consider it in your heart, that*

the LORD Himself is God in heaven above and on the earth beneath; *there is no other.* **Deuteronomy 4:32-39**

Verse 36 says *"out of heaven He let you hear His voice so that he might instruct you."* So they were able to hear on earth words from spoken from heaven.

God speaks all the time, He is speaking right now. There are various electronics signals in every room, the only reason you can't hear or see it is because you don't have the equipment. Similarly you need spiritual equipment to hear God speak because He speaks all the time. You know that the natural has no choice but to give way to what already exists in the spirit. The problem with many children of God is that we a purely declaring the things in the natural, we are not building in the spirit first.

An error in the church is people living a defeated lifestyle, a life meshed in poverty on earth and waiting to go to a place called heaven where the streets are paved with gold… this simply does not add up.

There is no point to a long life devoid of quality.. Living the days of heaven on earth means living on earth with lots of the qualities and the evidence that we are candidates of heaven and to illustrate this point we are examining the interactions between heaven and earth. To enjoy the days of heaven on earth there must be channels through which earth transacts business with heaven. We are now looking at Communication between heaven and earth. This involves written and verbal communication. Can God read? Can God write? Can God speak? Can we hear Him on earth when He speaks? These are vital questions.

It's important you understand that when talking of communication as an interaction between heaven and earth one of the things this does is, it changes your attitudes towards prayer. You become more aware that when you speak, God hears and when God speaks you hear. We need to live in the reality of His presence. We are constantly in God's presence twenty four hours and seven days a week. This should reflect in our conduct and confidence.

Also, we have to get rid of the thought that the House of God is represented by physical buildings. If you go round the UK today, you will see churches that were built with Christian donations decades ago; some are now residential houses, offices and some are Islamic centres. Hence if the building called "church" is the house of God, does that mean God is now homeless?

There is an overemphasis on the building. It is true it is not ideal to have meetings in the open. Buildings are merely functional. Lots of people felt that landed property was a house of God, and such properties are now occupied by demons. It's not about a building. It's about where God chooses to manifest His presence. The bible says *"thanks be to God the father of our Lord Jesus Christ who causes us to triumph and make manifest by us the fragrance of his Knowledge in every place"*. This means it does not matter where you are; on the train you are in church, in the supermarket, you are in church, at work you are in church. Anywhere you are, you carry the presence of God around with you.

If the queen of England moves into your house today, it becomes a palace even if you don't change anything in the building; because the palace is where the queen lives. So the queen gives meaning to the building. If the queen decides to leave Buckingham Palace and not live there anymore then it becomes like any other building. **It is important for you to understand that the place of the manifest presence of God is the house of God.** You carry God around with you everywhere you go. If you live in that reality then you can understand that you cannot just mouth-off anyhow thinking you are out of His presence. You have to constantly live in the reality of the presence of God.

God is not just God of heaven, but He is also God of the earth. In verse 36, it states, *"Out of heaven He let you hear His voice that He might instruct you"*. So they were able to hear on earth, words spoken from heaven. How is this possible? We need to go into the school of the Spirit for interpretation.

*"So there was great joy in Jerusalem: for since the time of Solomon the son of David king of Israel there was not the like in Jerusalem. Then the priests the Levites arose and blessed the people: and **their voice was heard, and their***

prayer came up to his holy dwelling place, even unto heaven". 2 Chronicles 30:26-27

People spoke on earth and God heard in heaven, what does this mean? It means there is an open channel between earth and heaven through our communication; so it is important for you to understand that the words of your mouth are more powerful than you think. That is why you can hardly have what you have not declared with your words. *"Thy will be done on earth, as it is in heaven."* The bible says the voice of their prayer was heard in Heaven in the holy habitation of God, and they were not dead. They did not die before the prayer and they did not die after the prayer and yet they interacted with heaven. Why do you think therefore that everything about you is purely earthly?

Do you remember the story of Hezekiah? After the nation was threatened; a letter was written to him telling him, "this is it, you have 24 hours before we wipe you out". The Bible says **Hezekiah took the letter to God and said** *"read it"* (literal interpretation). And God read the letter and responded. He said *"don't be afraid. I will deliver this nation, for My own sake, but also for the sake of my servant David".* The bible says in 24 hours one angel of the Lord destroyed over 185,000 Assyrians. **When God reads your letter, He acts based on what He has read.**

This is how Hezekiah got the letter and took it to God to read:

"Thus you shall speak to Hezekiah king of Judah, saying: 'Do not let your God in whom you trust deceive you, saying, "Jerusalem shall not be given into the hand of the king of Assyria." [11] *Look! You have heard what the kings of Assyria have done to all lands by utterly destroying them; and shall you be delivered?* [12] *Have the gods of the nations delivered those whom my fathers have destroyed, Gozan and Haran and Rezeph, and the people of Eden who were in Telassar?* [13] *Where is the king of Hamath, the king of Arpad, and the king of the city of Sepharvaim, Hena, and Ivah?'"* [14] *And Hezekiah **received the letter from the hand of the messengers, and read it;** and **Hezekiah went up to the house of the LORD, and <u>spread it before the LORD.</u>*** [15] *Then Hezekiah prayed before the LORD, and said: "O LORD God of Israel, the One who dwells between the cherubim, You are God, You alone, of all the kingdoms of the*

earth. You have made heaven and earth. **16** Incline Your ear, O LORD, and hear; **open Your eyes, O LORD, and see**; and hear the words of Sennacherib, which he has sent to reproach the living God. 2 Kings 19:10-16

After reading the letter, the Lord responded.

"Therefore thus says the LORD concerning the king of Assyria: 'He shall not come into this city, Nor shoot an arrow there, Nor come before it with shield, Nor build a siege mound against it. By the way that he came, By the same shall he return; And he shall not come into this city,' Says the LORD. ***'For I will defend this city, to save it. For My own sake and for My servant David's sake."*** *And it came to pass on a certain night that* ***the angel of the LORD went out, and killed in the camp of the Assyrians one hundred and eighty-five thousand;*** *and when people arose early in the morning, there were the corpses — all dead.* **36** *So Sennacherib king of Assyria departed and went away, returned home, and remained at Nineveh.* 2Kings 19:32-36

You receive a letter telling you that you will be sacked and you know that it is not God's will for this to happen, don't bother yourself, take the letter to God and ask Him to read it. This is what has been said. God acts based on what He reads.

You received a letter from the doctors saying you have cancer; don't worry, just take the letter before God and ask Him to read it. God can read and he speaks. He will respond like only He can. You need to begin to interact with God in ways like never before. Many times I have taken documents to God to show Him what has been said and God acted based on that. You need to understand that God reads and God speaks in ways like never before. So, communication is a key element to the interaction between heaven and earth. The Lord speaks all the time and we can hear Him clearly from the earth.

> *God's vision is for us to live the days of heaven on earth; both in terms of longevity and of course quality of life*

John Chapter 12 verse 24-30
"Verily, verily, I say unto you, Except a corn of wheat fall into the ground and die, it abideth alone: but if it die, it

bringeth forth much fruit. He that loveth his life shall lose it; and he that hateth his life in this world shall keep it unto life eternal. If any man serve me, let him follow me; and where I am, there shall also my servant be: if any man serve me, him will my Father honour. Now is my soul troubled; and what shall I say? Father, save me from this hour: but for this cause came I unto this hour. Father, glorify thy name. **Then came there a voice from heaven**...

Please note that Jesus was on earth when this was happening.

....*saying, I have both glorified it, and will glorify it again.* **The people therefore, that stood by, and heard it,** *said that it thundered: others said, An angel spake to him. Jesus answered and said, This voice came not because of me, but for your sakes"*.

Again, we see here that heaven spoke. Not only did Jesus hear it, but the people around Him also heard it. This is communication between heaven and earth. A key instrument of Dominion on earth is ability to communicate with heaven and hear from heaven. Without it; all you will have left are the earthly human wisdom and calculations which always ends in disaster.

When last did you hear the voice of God? Amongst the noises in our generation when last did you hear the voice of God? Many times, the noise is louder than the voice and many times so many of us are so engaged with the noise that we have forgotten the voice. Your ears will open from today; you will begin to ear God like never before in Jesus name.

Are you a voice or are you a noise? You are what you listen to. You become the voice you hear. If all you listen to is noise, then you become noise yourself. It's important for you to understand that God speaks. Men spoke on earth and God heard in heaven. God spoke in heaven and men heard on earth. Communication is a key interaction between heaven and earth. When you speak heaven will respond, from today you need to understand that you have the voice, the tool and the capability to change your circumstance, change the nations and cities you are in by listening to the voice of God and interacting between heaven and earth through your communication.

Chapter 3: Interactions between Heaven and Earth

I declare this all the time. Whenever I go into cities, I do simple things; the bible says *"the earth is the Lord's and the fullness thereof"*. That means God owns everything, but the kings of this world are in control of what God owns. The bible also says *"the heart of the kings are in the hands of the Lord, and He turns it in whichever way He wishes"* ; therefore I declare that *God now begins to turn their hearts in my favour. Therefore this land must respond to me differently and from this moment onwards kings must begin to bring the resources of this land that belong to God in the first place, my way.* And I begin to make those declarations. You need to understand clearly that things just don't happen. You declare it.

Interaction between heaven and earth. Before too long, the kings indeed begin to bring the resources your way. People do not do things for you because they like you, don't be fooled, even if they are relatives. As a matter of fact, have you ever wanted to start a business and you are depending on an uncle? You go to his house and he is giving people who are not related to him lots of money in your presence, but he is not even looking in your direction.

Until the hearts of kings are turned in your direction, you will not get anything. It's important for you to understand that God ultimately is your source. And who God uses becomes irrelevant. When you speak, Heaven will respond.

A FORETASTE OF HEAVEN

Let me be clear about something, and this is the fact that this book is by no means advocating over-spirituality and laziness....waiting for God to do things we can get up and do ourselves. It is about acting in the natural; after obtaining spiritual insight and revelation about an issue. I believe in the place called heaven. What I am saying is that we are supposed to have a foretaste of heaven while still here on earth. That is why we are looking at the various interactions between heaven and earth to establish this point. This is the only way we can live above the world's system and exercise dominion. We cannot have dominion on earth if all we do is dictated by earthly knowledge and limitations.

There is so much more for us to learn about interactions between heaven and earth. You possess spiritual weapons the world has never seen; when you stand in your place in God and make certain declarations in the spirit; then the world has no choice but to listen.

One of the things that happen once you understand these principles of interaction between heaven and earth is that you will indeed enter a rest, like the bible says, *"he that has entered the Lords rest, has ceased from his own works"*. In other words, what troubles others will not trouble you at all. You are not perturbed by what people do or say.

I remember a few years back while on a transatlantic flight; there was very bad turbulence on this particular flight. I was sitting next to the CEO of one of the global oil companies and I could see he was very petrified. I had to comfort him, telling him not to worry as nothing would happen. In astonishment, he asked how I knew and I responded "Because I am on board. I am your insurance policy. Nothing will happen"; I assured him. He clearly became interested in what I had to say for the rest of the flight. Why that audacity you may ask? Simply, it is called Divine Guidance. Divine guidance breeds divine confidence. When you are in obedience to the voice of the spirit, you are fully covered by heaven's guarantee.

I am trying to let you know there is interaction between heaven and earth, and during this interaction God speaks. What He says sometimes may not be comfortable; which is the difficulty with human beings, but you know you heard His voice, act on it. God guides.

THE TREE OF LIFE

Another key example I want to give to illustrate this point about how we need to live on earth based on heaven's resources is the tree of life.

There were three trees in the Garden of Eden:
1. All manner of trees
2. Tree of Life and
3. The tree of knowledge of good and evil

Those are the three categories of trees that the bible expressed. I will not go into how clearly God's plan was for man to eat of the tree of life, but of course man was too thick to get what God was saying. God set everything up and then zoomed in on two particular trees and said of one of them you should not eat. Even if you are half smart you will understand that what God is trying to say about the other one is to eat of it, but as in everything else, God won't force you. You have to choose the tree of life, but of course man did not.

We then read how God drove man out of the garden and put Angels to guard the entrance to the garden so that man could not go back and eat of the tree of life in his fallen state. The plan of God was for man to eat of the tree of life in his righteous, unfallen state – that way; man would have lived in that state perpetually.

Now with man in a fallen state, God decided to ensure he did not eat of the tree of life, as that would completely skew God's plans, because that would mean man would remain in his fallen state forever. Just as he would have remained in his righteous state forever before he sinned. God decided that man should be prevented from accessing that tree. So understanding and partaking of the tree of life will help us see what God's original intention was for creation.

There were two key security measures God put in place; the bible says the Angels had as weapons to guard the entrance to the garden. So, firstly the two Angels were there, they were the bouncers to ensure man did not go back into the garden and they secondly had a flaming sword, just in case man had any funny ideas. What do these things mean? Who are the Cherubims? They are one of the ministering spirits, sent to minister to the heirs of salvation we hear in the bible. When God sent His only begotten Son to the world He gave a command in Hebrews Chapter 1 verse 6.

> *Everything that truly exist on earth for a believer, is merely replicating something that exists in heaven*

"And again, when he bringeth in the firstbegotten into the world, he saith, And let all the angels of God worship him". Hebrews 1:6

Think about this; If Jesus had approached the entrance to the garden the cherubim would have moved out of the way and worship Him, based on the instructions above. So the key to allowing the Angels to allow you access is to go hand in hand with Jesus. So without Christ we cannot access the tree of life.

You have to be able to go past the cherubim. The only way man could get past the Cherubim was if he went hand-in-hand with Jesus, because not for man's sake, but for His sake, when the cherubim see Him, they will have no choice but to worship Him. And this means therefore that the way back to the tree of life is first of all through salvation. **Without Christ, it is impossible to access the tree of life.** You have to be saved, "Let all angels worship him" means the only way you can go pass the cherubims is if Christ is holding your hand while you walk pass.

Chapter 4: A Foretaste of Heaven

If you go to the White House in the USA and the President is holding your hand and taking you round; all the guards will be saluting him and granting him access. It's not you they are saluting but him. But because the president is there with you, they will open doors for him to go through that you could not have gone through by yourself. You are able to access everywhere he can access because you are with him.

Do you know that if the current president holds your hand and is on his way to a top secret briefing, that briefing will still have to proceed, even though you are there and you may not be fully vetted yet? The fact that the president is there and approves overrides everything. He is the Commander in Chief. In America for instance, they have certain classified information, some can never be declassified and some only after 30 or 50 year; but any document in the US can be declassified in an instant by a Presidential order. It does not matter what classification a document is, if the President says he wants the nation to know about it, from that moment the document becomes declassified. You will be able to access things you could not otherwise access on your own because you are with the President. Similarly, Jesus grants us access to the tree of life.

The second layer of security is the flaming sword: Through Jesus we have passed through the Cherubim, how do we pass through the flaming sword?

"For the word of God is quick, and powerful, and sharper than any two edged sword" Hebrews 4:12.

From this scripture, we know the sword therefore, is the word of God. The bible says Flaming Sword. If you read Jeremiah chapter 20, verse 9 the bible talks about the word of God being like "fire shut up in my bones"

"Then I said, I will not make mention of him, nor speak any more in his name. But his word was in mine heart as a burning fire shut up in my bones, and I was weary with forbearing, and I could not stay" Jeremiah 20:9

If you have accepted Jesus into your life and He is your Lord and you declare the word of God then you can access the tree of life. This means that to find our way back to the tree of life which was God's original intended purpose, we need to go through these two stage security.

Now, I want to show you what was contained in the tree of life that God wanted man to partake of in the first instance. This is to further demonstrate the interactions between heaven and earth. If man had done this, it would have consolidated God' plan. But God took out an insurance policy, because the bible says "the Lamb of God was slain before the foundations of the earth".

Before and after the fall, the tree of life is significant. Man was supposed to partake of the tree of life before he sinned and after he had sinned God still wanted him to partake of the tree of life, but to do that you now have to go through the two stage security we have just looked at.

The other pertinent question is, what happened to the tree of life when flood destroyed the earth? We knew it was in the garden, that's why the cherubims were protecting it. **If God intended that man would never partake of the tree of life again, He would never have**

put the cherubim there to protect the tree in the Garden, He would have simply uprooted it. That way it would have been a done deal. But He still left the tree there and was protecting it which showed that God still wants man to partake of it. But after the flood destroyed everything, what happened to the tree of Life. The tree of life that was here on earth was transplanted into heaven and man through interactions between heaven and earth has to partake of the tree of life.

"And he showed me a pure river of water of life, clear as crystal, proceeding from the throne of God and of the Lamb. ² *In the middle of its street, and* ***on either side of the river, was the tree of life****, which bore twelve fruits, each tree yielding its fruit every month. The leaves of the tree were for the healing of the nations.* ³ *And there shall be no more curse, but the throne of God and of the Lamb shall be in it, and His servants shall serve Him"*. Revelation 22:1-3

In the above scripture; there were two trees of life; one on either side of the river. Nothing Godly exists on earth without it first of all existing in heaven. **What substantiates and sustains what is on earth is the fact that it is a physical reproduction of what exists in**

heaven. The tree of life would not exist on earth if there was no tree of life in heaven. So when the tree of life that was on earth was transplanted to heaven; that is why heaven now had two trees of life.

Everything that exists on earth for a believer, is merely replicating something that exists in heaven. That is why if you read Revelation Chapter 11, it talks about the temple of God, the Ark of God and even earthquakes in heaven, because the only way things happen on earth is if they are a model of what is in heaven. The spiritual controls the physical. **The tree of life was transplanted to heaven, but it was returned back to earth not as a tree but as Jesus. So that if we partake of Him, then God's original plan will still be consummated.**

The other thing in Revelation chapter 22 verse 2 is:
*"....the tree of life, which **bare twelve manner of fruits**, and yielded her fruit every month: and the leaves of the tree were for the healing of the nations"*

The tree was bearing 12 different types of fruit. This was not natural, because every tree is supposed to produce after its own kind, an apple tree is supposed to produce apples and an orange tree, oranges. But the bible says there is a tree here that has 12 manners of fruits on one tree.

We need to go into the school of the Spirit for interpretation. One tree, 12 fruits; one loin 12 tribes of Israel. The bible says the leaf of the tree was for the healing of the nations. Twelve is God's number of Government. *"The Government shall be upon His shoulders"*.

Some key facts:
"Now when He had taken the scroll, the four living creatures and the twenty-four elders fell down before the Lamb, each having a harp, and golden bowls full of incense, which are the prayers of the saints". Revelation 5:8

These twenty-four elders represent the twelve tribes of Israel and the twelve apostles of the Lamb. Four living creatures in their midst. The bible says a river went out of Eden, Eastward of Eden and parted into four heads. The word of God has four dimensions: It's alive; It's powerful; it's sharper than any two edged sword and it pierces up to the marrow. Also the word of God has four applications. It is profitable for Doctrine, Reproof, Correction and Instructions in righteousness.

Twelve tribes came out of one man, but we also know they had four mothers. These numbers are no accident. Four wives, Rachael, Leah, Zilpah and Bilha. Restoration in the bible must be four-fold, 2 Samuel chapter 12. (Fourfold restoration David declared).

"And when Jesus came to the place, he looked up, and saw him, and said unto him, Zacchaeus, make haste, and come down; for to day I must abide at thy house. And he made haste, and came down, and received him joyfully. And when they saw it, they all murmured, saying, That he was gone to be guest with a man that is a sinner. And Zacchaeus stood, and said unto the Lord: Behold, Lord, the half of my goods I give to the

> *The difficulty with many of us as children of God is that we are purely declaring in the natural*

*poor; and if I have taken any thing from any man by false accusation, I **restore him fourfold**".* Luke 19: 5 – 8.

If the tree of Life in the Garden was transplanted to heaven how do we here on earth now partake of it? Where is the exact location of the tree of Life in heaven? Who qualifies to eat of it? What are the representations of the tree of live today to the believer?

We have already discussed that there are three types of trees in the garden:
1. All manner of trees
2. the Tree of life
3. Tree of the knowledge of good and evil

There were three trees on Calvary. Jesus was in the middle and a thief on either side, both of them on a tree.

"He that hath an ear, let him hear what the Spirit saith unto the churches; To him that overcometh will I give to eat of the tree of life, which is in the midst of the paradise of God". Revelation Chapter 2:7

When one of the thieves told Jesus "remember me when you are in your kingdom" what was Jesus' response? Jesus said *"Today, you will be with me in paradise"*. Where is this? Where is the tree of life we have just read about. In the paradise of God. Where is this? And how do you get into that paradise?

When you stand in your place in God and make certain declarations, then the world has no choice but to listen. You go into the secret place of the spirit, you hear the voice of God, you make certain declarations in the spirit and then you come into the physical and begin to see those things come into manifestation and people begin to wonder where you are coming from? You need to understand that once what you want is already established in the Spirit, you can boldly come into the natural and declare it because you know that the natural has no choice but to give way to what already exists in the spirit.

The difficulty with many of us as children of God is that we are purely declaring in the natural, we are not building things in the Spirit first. And because we are declaring it in the natural we are fighting in the terrain and with tools the enemy can easily deflect. It is important for you to understand that God wants us to enjoy the days of heaven on earth and one of the tools through which we will do this is through understanding what the tree of life represents in our day? We know that there are fruits of the tree of knowledge of good and evil which man partook of, we will see how this relates to the tree of life and how we can use this in terms of interactions between heaven and earth. There is no way you can exercise dominion on earth without partaking of the tree of life. It is just impossible.

EATING OF THE TREE OF LIFE

Who you are in Christ is not so much about what you say; it's about who you are within. What you have within you. In the preceding chapter, we have been looking at the tree of life and I used the tree of life as an illustration of interaction between heaven and earth.

After Christ was resurrected from the dead, the bible says the women came and wanted to touch but he told them not to because He had a different body. However in that same body he showed himself to the disciples. And when he got to them he asked them what food they had, and he ate with them. You would have thought in that glorified body he would not be able to eat on earth, he should eat strictly in heaven;

but this shows the interaction between heaven and earth, as heaven is not a place you have to die to experience. Before you get there in person, you can also get there spiritually because it should inform your quality of life here on earth. This is the basis for dominion. When everyone says there is a casting down, you will be able to say there is a lifting up.

Genesis 1:26, God said *let us make man in our image and after our likeness,* but after man fell in Gen. 3:22, the bible says God said **"man has become like one of us"**. This does not make sense as man was made in God's image originally. Man has become like one of them, if man was like them then every part will be in alignment with each other, in total unity, and harmony and agreement. This means before the fall, man's spirit, soul and body walked in unison just like the trinity, but when man sinned the soul died spiritually and there was a disconnection between the spirit and body, so man was no longer in complete alignment like "them" because man had now become like "one" instead of three in one. So man became "one" of us; rather than "one of us". Man became like "one" of them. The question is which one, The one that will know sin, the one that was slain before the foundations of the earth, the one that became sin for us.

We now want to discuss what the tree of life represents. So I am going to use the word "fruit" for ease of understanding. The tree of knowledge of good and evil has its own fruit. These are:
1. Deception
2. Lust of the flesh
3. Lust of the eyes
4. Pride of life

Once you fall into deception, all the other fruits come rushing in and that is what happened in Genesis chapter 3. If a tree does not bear any fruit from a distance it's difficult to know what kind of tree it is, if you are an expert, maybe from the leaves you might be able to know what kind of tree it is. From a distance, if you can't see any fruit and you see three trees side by side, it may be difficult for you to know which one is which. The bible says by their fruit you shall know them, what evidence do you have as a believer, if you don't have any fruit to show. That's why believers who do not bear fruit are not easily identified as Christians or followers of Christ. It's by their fruit you shall know them, and not by their title.

WHAT DOES THE TREE OF LIFE REPRESENT TO US TODAY?

*Happy is the man that findeth **wisdom**, and the man that getteth understanding. For the merchandise of it is better than the merchandise of silver and the gain thereof than fine gold. She is more precious than rubies: and all the things thou canst desire are not to be compared unto her. Length of days is in her right hand; and in her left hand riches and honour. Her ways are ways of pleasantness and all her paths are peace. **She is a tree of life to them that lay hold upon her**: and happy is everyone that retaineth her.* Proverbs 3:13

The first representation of the tree of life is Wisdom. This is the first thing that the tree of life represents to us today. This was God's intention to start with; when man was living before the fall, he was supposed to live with wisdom had he eaten of the tree of life in his unfallen state. And everything we are now chasing after are things that were part of God's original package, that man lost when sin came.

"But of him are ye in Christ Jesus, who of God is made unto us wisdom and righteousness and sanctification and redemption". 1 Corinthians 1:30

You can see why Christ had to become wisdom for us, because He was the last Adam that came and what Christ restored were the things man should have partaken of if he had eaten of the tree of life before he fell, because God knew we needed the tree of life to be able to interact between heaven and earth accurately. But when man fell he lost that opportunity, and when Christ came, He came to restore the tree of life. In other words we are partaking of the tree of life but not in a literal sense of fruit now, but through Christ. This is why He became Wisdom for us.

> *After you understand Dominion; when everyone says there is a casting down, you will be able to say there is a lifting up*

Wisdom is a tree of life.

The important thing here is between the wisdom of Christ and the wisdom of Solomon which one is greater? If the wisdom of Solomon received all the gold of Sheba, how much more would the Wisdom of Christ? Why are we walking around deprived when we are supposed to walk in wisdom? It is important to realise that unless you understand wisdom is a tree of life, you will not understand that demonstrating wisdom in the things of life, is evidence of the interaction between heaven and earth. It shows that you are not looking at things purely from an earthly view. Christ has become wisdom for us which means you have to be saved to have that wisdom.

*"He that troubleth his own house shall inherit the wind and the fool shall be servant to the wise of heart. **The fruit of the righteous is a tree of life;** and he that winneth souls is wise"*. Proverbs 11:29

The second thing that the tree of life represents to us is **the Fruit of the Righteous**. What is the fruit of the righteous? The **fruit** of the righteous is not quite the same thing as **fruits** of righteousness. **The fruit of the**

righteous is the resources of the righteous. Let us allow scriptures to interpret scripture.

*"But this I say, He which soweth sparingly shall reap also sparingly; and he which soweth bountifully shall reap also bountifully. Every man according as he purposeth in his heart, so let him give; not grudgingly or of necessity: for God loveth a cheerful giver. And God is able to make all grace abound toward you; that ye always having all sufficiency in all things, may abound to every good work. As it is written, He that dispersed abroad; he hath given to the poor; his righteousness remaineth for ever. Now he that ministereth seed to the sower both minister read for your food, and multiply your seed sown, and increase the **fruits of your righteousness**"*. 2 Corinthians 9:6

What is Paul talking about here?

*"For I long to see you, that I may impart unto you some spiritual gift, to the end ye may be established; that is, that I may be comforted together with you by the mutual faith both of you and me. Now I would not have you ignorant, brethren, that often times I purposed to come unto you (but was let hitherto,) that I might **have some <u>fruit</u> among you** also, even as among other Gentiles"*. Romans 1:11

*"For which cause also I have been much hindered from coming to you, but now having no more place in these parts, and having a great desire these many years to come unto you. Whensoever I take my journey into Spain, I will come to you for I trust to see you in my journey, and to be brought on my way thitherward by you, if first I be somewhat filled with your company. But now I go unto Jerusalem to minister unto the saints. For it hath pleased them of Macedonia and Achaia to make a **certain contribution for the poor** saints which are at Jerusalem. It hath pleased them verily and their debtors they are. For if the Gentiles have been made partakers of their spiritual things, their duty is also to minister unto them in carnal things. When therefore I have performed this, and **have sealed to them <u>this fruit</u>**, I will come by you in Spain"*. Romans 15:22

"But I rejoiced in the Lord greatly that now at the last your care of me hath flourished again; wherein ye were also careful, but ye lacked opportunity. Not that I speak in respect of want; for I have learned in whatsoever state I am, therewith to be content. I know both how to be abased, and I know how to abound; everywhere and in all things I am instructed both to be full and to be hungry, both to abound and to suffer need. I can do all things through Christ who

Chapter 5: Eating of the Tree of Life

*strengthens me. Notwithstanding, ye have well done, that ye did communicate with my affliction. Now ye Philippians know also that in the beginning of the gospel, when I departed from Macedonia no church communicated with me as **concerning giving and receiving** but ye only. For even in Thessalonica ye sent once and again unto my necessity. Not because I desire a gift but **I desire <u>fruit</u> that may abound to your account**".* Philippians 4:10

The fruit of the righteous is the resources of the righteous; a man who is committed to investing in the kingdom of God is a man who has eaten of the tree of life. The fruit of the righteous is a tree of life; you eat of the fruit of life as a righteous man. One of the things God wanted settled, is that when man is on earth to live, he lives with the resources of heaven. If man had not fallen we would not have all the problems we have today, the bible says there is a river that flows east out of Eden and the river parted into four heads, the first head was revealing gold, the gold that we now have to dig hard to find; was once freely available. In other words things we are struggling for will become very easy if we partake of the tree of life. Therefore rather than sweating silly, toiling and making nothing, if you partake of the tree of life, it's one of the evidences of the interaction between heaven and earth then you will be able to see beyond the natural. What we are struggling for is available in Christ Jesus if we know how to engage the interaction between heaven and earth.

Christ has become wisdom for us. Ability to deal with affairs of life wisely and see things where others don't see. When everyone is worried about things and you are at peace. So **the second fruit** of the tree of life is the fruit of the righteous, i.e., your resources. Imagine how foolish it is when man tries to hide his resources from God. Because the fruit of the righteous, the bible says in Proverbs 11:30 is a tree of life.

"A soft answer turns away wrath, But a harsh word stirs up anger. [2] *The tongue of the wise uses knowledge rightly, But the mouth of fools pours forth foolishness.* [3] *The eyes of the LORD are in every place, Keeping watch on the evil and the good.* [4] ***A wholesome tongue is a tree of life****, But perverseness in it breaks the spirit"*. Proverbs 15:1-4

The third thing that the tree of life represents to us is **a Wholesome Tongue.** It's not strange that Solomon's wisdom is what has revealed all these things.

Are you a person of your word? Do you give life through your words or do filthy words proceed out of your mouth all the time. A wholesome tongue is a tree of life, because just like God spoke the heavens and the earth into existence, we who are created in His image are supposed to bring things into existence by our words, and that is why it is important to understand that for your tongue to be a tree of life, then it has to be a tongue that is saying the word of God.

When the tongue is guided by the Spirit of God, it can impart truth and elicit thoughts which will be valuable to those who come under their influence. God planted the tree of life in the Garden of Eden (Gen. 2:9), and whoever ate from it would find life. Today, we find the tree of life in the wholesome speech that flows out from a man's tongue. An unwholesome tongue on the other hand brings forth death. The Bible commands, *"Do not let any unwholesome talk come out of your mouths, but only what is helpful for building others up according to their needs, that it may benefit those who listen"* (Eph. 4:29, NIV).

Stop using your mouth to speak negative words. Learn to say the right words. Be a person of your word. Saying and not meaning it or saying something and not doing it is wrong. One of the things we as Christians are guilty of is saying things like "**I am are praying for you**" almost as if we are comforting people but the truth is are you really praying for them? You know you have not prayed for that person. A wholesome tongue is a tree of life. For you to partake of interactions between heaven and earth having a wholesome tongue is very important. Morgan Freeman acted the part of God in a movie "Bruce Almighty". And in the movie a man was given the power to be "God" for a period of time. One of the things he noticed was that he was saying things carelessly and they were happening, he would think things and changes would take place. Suddenly it

> *The kingdom of God is all about you starting and finishing well.*

occurred to him that having the power meant he could not just say or think anything he liked because, by virtue of the fact that he was "God" whatever he said or thought would happen. It became too much for him to handle the power. So the man begged God (Freeman) to take back the powers.

For you to be able to interact effectively between heaven and earth, you have to learn to use your wholesome tongue properly. Jesus when he was at the tomb of Lazarus, was quite specific when He said "Lazarus come forth". If He had simply said "come forth", all the dead buried in the tombs would have all come forth. Once you learn to use your words effectively then you need to know that whatever you say will come to pass. Do not let any careless words proceed out of your mouth. How can you look at a sick person and say "in Jesus name be healed" at 10:00 and at 10:05 use the same mouth to abuse someone else. How do you think the angels will differentiate what you are saying? If the power is there, it's there. It's either there is zero power in your words, in which case you are in great difficulty or indeed if there is power in your word as a child of God then what you say comes to pass.

It's important that we learn to control what we say because **the more control you have over your words the more power God can entrust you with.** God will not turn you loose on the world with such power in your words only for you to be carelessly pronouncing things anyhow. It's important that for God to trust you with His power in your word then you have got to be careful what you say.

Lastly, Proverbs Chapter 13 verse 11-12. *"Wealth gotten by vanity shall be diminished: but he that gathereth by labour shall increase. Hope deferred maketh the heart sick; but **when the desire cometh, it is a tree of life**"*.

Desire accomplished or purpose fulfilled is a tree of life.

Psalm 20 verses 4 and 5: *"Grant thee according to thine own heart, and fulfil all they counsel. We will rejoice in thy salvation and in the name of our God we will set up our banners; the Lord fulfil all thy petitions"*.

Desire accomplished is a tree of life. This means the hallmark of a man who is walking with reality of the interactions between heaven and earth, is ability to finish and finish strong. Don't let your life be a symbol of abandoned projects. Anybody can do anything for a few days, the questions is how do you sustain what you started. It's very important that you sustain your enthusiasm for more than two or three days. The grace is on your life as a child of God not only to start things but also to finish what you have started and finish strong, that is your inheritance. This is why the bible says, *"he that puts his hand on the plough and looks back is not fit for the kingdom of God"*.

The kingdom of God is all about you starting and finishing well. Desire accomplished or purpose fulfilled is a tree of life. There is a tree of life on earth and one in heaven and nothing exists on earth that did not first exist in heaven and how after the fall of man, the tree of life on earth was transplanted to heaven and that is why in Revelation we saw that there were two trees of life on either side of the river. It is important to see therefore that when talking about interactions between heaven and earth, partaking of the tree of life is one of those interactions because the tree of life exists in heaven and as we said *"thy will be done on earth as it is in heaven"*.

The things we are looking at the moment are by no means the limit to the interactions between heaven and earth. We are supposed to live the days of heaven on earth and this means we are able to live on earth with our connections still in heaven. This is the meaning of dominion living.

I have a friend who used to be in the US military, who told me they have a base here in the UK. In that base, according to him, they mainly spend dollars and not pounds. All the shops on the base are mainly shops that exist in the US, in other words it's a mini United States in the UK. This is done so that when the soldiers return home there is less adjustment to be made. They repeat this in all US military bases around the world, he said. When abroad they spend the same type of money, buy the same type of products and by the time they get home they continue as normal and there is less adjustment needed.

Chapter 5: Eating of the Tree of Life

In discussing interactions between heaven and earth, just as we know we will eventually return home which is heaven, but before we get home we want to familiarise ourselves with home in such a way that when we get there, we will go with the flow easily. There will be less adjustments. Living the days of heaven on earth is exactly like this. It's like living in the US military base in the UK, that looks and feels like living in the US.

> *When you have access to everything heaven has; Nothing on this earth should limit you*

HEAVEN'S TRANSPORTATION SYSTEM

Living on earth with the resources of heaven behind you is what dominion is about. To evidence this, we have so far looked at some interactions between heaven and earth.

On earth there are different forms and types of transportation; air, sea, rail etc. In heaven; transportation system is the easiest; all you need is for

God to open your eyes and say *"come up here"*. Death is not the only way to interact with heaven. You will short-change yourself if you think you need to die to experience heaven.

In 2 Corinthians Chapter 12 Paul explains his experience in the Third Heavens, he called it paradise. How did he get there? What was his mode of transportation? In Revelation Chapter 4, John was in the spirit in the Lords day and immediately he was in heaven. How did he get there? In Acts Chapter 8 Phillip was having a wonderful time with the Samaritans doing the work of God, he was then told by the angel of the Lord that he should go to a desert place to baptize one person – The Ethiopian Eunuch. When he got there he finished the task and the bible says Phillip vanished from his presence and the next time we see him he was at Azotus. **How was he transported?** This is heaven's transportation system at work. What is the transportation system in heaven? You can live beyond the limits of this world. You are a supernatural being in a natural capsule called body. Express yourself.

Chapter 5: Eating of the Tree of Life

"But an angel of the Lord spoke to Philip saying, "Arise and go south to the road that descends from Jerusalem to Gaza." (This is a desert road.) 27 And he arose and went; and behold, there was an Ethiopian eunuch, a court official of Candace, queen of the Ethiopians, who was in charge of all her treasure; and he had come to Jerusalem to worship. 28 And he was returning and sitting in his chariot, and was reading the prophet Isaiah. 29 And the Spirit said to Philip, "Go up and join this chariot." 30 And when Philip had run up, he heard him reading Isaiah the prophet, and said, "Do you understand what you are reading?" 31 And he said, "Well, how could I, unless someone guides me?" And he invited Philip to come up and sit with him. 32 Now the passage of Scripture which he was reading was this: "HE WAS LED AS A SHEEP TO SLAUGHTER; AND AS A LAMB BEFORE ITS SHEARER IS SILENT, SO HE DOES NOT OPEN HIS MOUTH. 33"IN HUMILIATION HIS JUDGMENT WAS TAKEN AWAY; WHO SHALL RELATE HIS GENERATION? FOR HIS LIFE IS REMOVED FROM THE EARTH."

34 And the eunuch answered Philip and said, "Please tell me, of whom does the prophet say this? Of himself, or of someone else?" 35 And Philip opened his mouth, and beginning from this Scripture he preached Jesus to him. 36 And as they went along the road they came to some water; and the eunuch said, "Look! Water! What prevents me from being baptized?" 37 38 And he ordered the chariot to stop; and they both went down into the water, Philip as well as the eunuch; and he baptized him. 39 And when they came up out of the water, **the Spirit of the Lord snatched**

Philip away; and the eunuch saw him no more, *but went on his way rejoicing. 40 But Philip found himself at Azotus; and as he passed through he kept preaching the gospel to all the cities, until he came to Caesarea".* Acts 8:26-40

People like George Lucas, copied from the bible, in films like Star Trek, where people vanish and appear elsewhere instantly. It's not original to Hollywood. People transported this way is heaven's technology. It can happen to you as it did to the apostles? Can we experience this today? Yes. Have you found yourself through dreams, in places you have never been physically? Knowing a venue without actually being there; a mental picture has been created in your imagination. I have had dreams about places that are so real in terms of description that should I visit there I will recognise it. If you have found yourself in dreams in places where you have never been physically, then you are tapping into the transportation system in heaven while you are here on earth.

Being in places you have never been in revelation and dreams is experiencing heavens transportation system. That is how heaven puts you in a place where you have physically not been but you act as though you have been there. That is what happened to Apostle Paul, He was not at the mount of transfiguration, but he knew a lot of things about what happened to Jesus even though he was not one of the original 12 disciples. How did he know? Heaven's transportation system. Spiritual transportation is one of the interactions between heaven and earth and an expression of our dominion on earth. We get a taste of heavens timeless flow and movement. There is no distance in the spirit. The Holy Spirit is the enabler of interaction between heaven and earth, and in spiritual transportation; visions, revelations and dreams are the three vehicles mostly used.

This allows us to experience the invisible and connect heaven to earth. The transportation system between heaven and earth is through visions, revelations and dreams. You begin to see places you have never been before. You begin to see things you did not even know existed. It could be months, days or years later that you will come into contact with those things and realise what you saw. You can also have a vision or a dream of something happening to someone else.

Heaven's transportation system can take you to places and see or hear things in the spirit through dreams, visions and revelations.

This is interaction between heaven and earth. How God can transport you into a situation that has absolutely nothing to do with you and begin to reveal to you things that are happening in other peoples' lives as though you are physically there. When this begins to happen this is an interaction between heaven and earth. You are being transported spiritually speaking even though physically you have not moved anywhere else; it is important that you yield yourself to God and allow Him to use you in ways like never before.

When the bible says we can live the days of heaven on earth, it is not a theory, or a promise that will go unfulfilled. It is something we need to take seriously. Investment and financial decisions that are made based on heaven's revelation will lead to certain wealth and abundance. Divine guidance produces divine prosperity. God's man, doing God's work, at

Chapter 5: Eating of the Tree of Life

God's time, in God's way, will NEVER lack God's resources.

You have access to everything heaven has. Nothing on this earth should limit you. Don't live your life as if all you have is all that is around you here on earth. Don't limit yourself in terms of what you hear. You as an individual do not have to go through the various seasons, because God can change times and seasons for you. The sun stood still for Joshua, there is no limit to you if you have interactions between heaven and earth. You have a choice, you can determine seasons or even change seasons; that is your prerogative as a child of God. Stop short-changing yourself. It's time for the manifestation of the true sons of God.

Note and Review

ENTERING INTO GOD'S REST

Heaven and earth have a link. The earth has its limitations but this has nothing to do with how far you go. The earth is governed by law and when a greater law comes to intervene the superior law takes over. There is the law of gravity which dictates that anything that goes up must come down, but within the earthly realm there is a law of lift which keeps an aeroplane in the sky.

The superior law overrides the previous inferior law. In the same way on earth when limitations come, rather than bother yourself, you just use the principles of interaction between heaven and earth; and then you can draw down from heavens resources and begin to move forward. You are unstoppable.

This is what makes you different from the unbeliever, when an unbeliever hits a road block that's it; they have nowhere to turn to, whereas you can go where it matters and change things and cause the physical change to take place. I want us to look at a few more instruments of dominion on earth. This point can never be overemphasised. I want us to look at **the watchers.**

*"Except the Lord build the house, they labour in vain that build it; except the Lord keep the city, **the watchman waketh but in vain"**.* Psalm 127:1

Who is the watchman? This is not your security guard. There are watchmen both in heaven and on earth. I am trying to show you that God requires two places where he can feel at home, and the standard in one will not be different from the other, God expects the same level of comfort in both homes, for that to take place there has to be a way of communicating and interacting between one and the other. This is important because in the world you will begin to see the shallowness and the substitute that other people have believed in this area.

Many believe that the only way we can experience heaven is when we die. I have already shown you that many people have interacted with heaven without dying. If we need to die to experience heaven, then why does the bible say we can live the days of heaven on earth? It's important for you to understand that you can experience heaven before you get to heaven. You need to understand that you are not limited by earthly infrastructure in terms of your ability to make headway here on earth.

THE WATCHERS FROM HEAVEN'S STANDPOINT

Thinking of Nebuchadnezzar, why did God not intervene when he was building the golden image? God waited till the image was ready and he had called all ends of the earth to come and celebrate his golden image. Then three Hebrew boys decided not to bow and we saw how the dedication never took place.

Because after the experience of throwing three people into the fire and seeing four people and the fourth was like the Son of God; something changed.

When they brought the three Hebrew boys out, Nebuchadnezzar declared that no other God should be worshiped except their God. And he proclaimed punishment on any one who worshipped any other god. The whole incident was to make people worship his golden image and suddenly by divine intervention the topic changed.

God is never too late, He shows up at the right time. You may be going through certain situations and asking God why He has not shown up yet. He always shows up at the right time. We are wondering why God does not intervene early in certain situations,

> *You need to understand that God will clean his temple, because you don't see them does not meant they don't exist*

sometimes God waits but when He shows up, He takes over.

In Daniel 4:1; Nebuchadnezzar the king to all peoples, nations and languages that dwell in all the earth, "peace be multiplied unto you". He was talking to everyone under the sphere of his influence.

"I saw in the visions of my head upon my bed, and behold, ***a watcher, a holy one, came down from heaven"****. This watcher is a heavenly being. "He cried aloud and said thus, Hew down the tree, and cut off his branches, shake off his leaves, and scatter his fruit; let the beasts get away from under it, and the fowls from his branches. Nevertheless leave the stump of his roots in the earth even with a band of iron and brass, in the tender grass of the field; and let it be wet with the dew of heaven, and let his portion be with the beasts in the grass of the earth". "Let his heart be changed from man's, and let a beast's heart be given unto him; and let seven times pass over him. This matter is by decree of the watchers and the sentence by the word of the Holy one in order that the living may know that the Most High lives in the Kingdom of men and giveth it to whomsoever he will and setteth up over it the basest of men"*. Daniel 4:13-17

The watchers here passed a decree that affected Nebuchadnezzar. So we can see that there are watchers that God sent from heaven. We don't know if they are angels from heavens perspective. They could be but the important thing here is that we know that there are watchers in heaven. If there are watchers in heaven, then by parallel, there must be watchers on earth.

WATCHERS FROM AN EARTHLY STAND POINT

"He cried also in mine ears with a loud voice, saying "Cause them that have charge over the city to draw near, even every man with his destroying weapon in his hand. And behold six men came from the way of the higher gate, which lieth toward the north, and every man a slaughter weapon in his hand; and one man among them was clothed with linen with a writers ink horn by his side; and they went in, and stood beside the brazen alter. And the glory of the God of Israel was gone up from the cherub, whereupon he was, to the threshold of the house and he called to the man clothed with linen who had the writers' inkhorn by his side. And the Lord said unto him, Go through the midst of Jerusalem and set a mark upon the foreheads of the men that sigh and that cry for all the abominations that be done in the midst

thereof. And to the others he said in my hearing "Go ye after him through the city, and smite: let not your eye spare, neither have ye pity; slay utterly old and young, both maids and little children, and women: but come not near any man upon whom is the mark; and begin at my sanctuary".
Ezekiel 9:1-6

They began with the elders who were before the temple. The men sent were the watchers. You need to understand that God will clean his temple, because you don't see them does not meant they don't exist, God has his watchers on earth and heaven taking record and pronouncing the mind of God to the people.

Watchers from an earthly stand point have a prophetic voice and authority to declare truth to power and to change the course of events in nations. The watchers on earth are human beings like you and I. They are people that God has given the prophetic grace to declare, they have power to change seasons. On the normal basis there is winter, summer, autumn and spring; however the question is what was the weather like in the wilderness was during the 40 years when the Israelites were there. **A pillar of cloud by day and pillar of fire by night, that was the weather** but what happened to the normal weather conditions? Also when the prophet came and said there shall be no rain except by his word, and there was no rain for a few years. What happened to the rainy season those years?

The watchers have power to change seasons, they have power to change what men and women are used to. They have power to change what physically human beings are used to. They are men and women of God that God uses in a profound way and God has put his word in their mouth and in every generation God will not leave himself without a witness. There are those who are currently watchers here on earth. That God has given the responsibility to declare true to power and to declare the truth of the word of God over the people.

God raised watchers on earth as he did in heaven. The warning finger of a prophet could be the declaration of an earthly watchman raised by God. Just as there are watchmen in heaven so there are on earth

*"Again the word of the Lord came unto me saying "Son of man speak to the children of thy people, (this is speaking of the instruction to the earthly watcher) and say unto them, when I bring the sword upon a land, if the people of the land take a man of their coasts and **set him for their watchman.** If when he seeth the sword come upon the land, he blow the trumpet and warn the people; then whomsoever heareth the sound of the trumpet and taketh not warning; if the sword come and take him away, his blood shall be upon his own head. He heard the sound of the trumpet but took not warning; his blood shall be upon him. But he that taketh warning shall deliver his soul. But if **the watchman** see the sword come, and blow not the trumpet, and the people be not warned; if the sword come, and take any person from among them, he is taken away to his iniquity; but his blood will I require at the **watchman's** hand. So thou, **son of man, I have made thee a watchman unto the house of Israel**; therefore thou shalt hear the word at my mouth and warn them from me"*. Ezekiel 33:1-7

Just as there are watchmen in heaven there are watchmen on earth. God said I have made thee a watchman for the house of Israel; therefore you shall hear a word from my mouth and shall warn them from me. Now you can see why some people, based on the gift of God in their heart, can't help but declare some things because as you have seen if they don't declare what the Lord has told them and then something happens to the nation or to the people, the bible says they will be held responsible because they have failed to declare God's word.

> *Enter His rest based on what you receive in heaven and suddenly nothing on earth seems to perturb you anymore.*

I have made you a watchman over Israel. We saw earlier a watchman coming down from heaven in the book of Daniel. We see how God says he has appointed us watchmen here on earth. God has his watchers on earth. They are taking records and pronouncing the mind of God

The watchers in heaven do come to earth and those on earth are given a glimpse of heaven from time to time. This is what enables them to declare boldly what they have seen and heard. That is another example of interactions between heaven and earth.

The watcher is common to both heaven and earth. To put this in picture sense, you will understand that nothing exists in the natural here on earth that does not exist spiritually. Since God created both places for his pleasure He has also designated to them watchers, the decrees they make are strong, that is why the prophet could say there would be no rain by his word, and it was only after he pronounced it that he went to talk to God about it. God did not tell him to make that declaration; he looked at the situation and pronounced a judgement over the situation and God stood by the word of His own Watcher. God chooses his watchers on earth and in heaven and there is communication between heaven and earth.

ENTER INTO GOD'S REST

"And on the seventh day, God ended His work which He had made; and He rested on the seventh day from all His work which He had made. Then God blessed the seventh day and sanctified it; because that in it He had rested from all

His work which God created and made". Genesis 2:1-3

After six days of creation, God rested. Is God a man? Does He get tired? Why did He need to rest? Does God need resting and refreshing? Is God Jesus? Did Jesus sleep on a pillow in the midst of a storm? Confusion comes from Psalm 121 verse 4 when the Bible says *"He that keeps Israel does not sleep nor slumber"*. This is what confuses a lot of people when you ask them this question. But there are dimension of God we are yet to fully appreciate. Clearly Rest in this dimension does not mean sleep. Rest takes place when a work is completed in the spirit. This enables ease and restful patience for the physical manifestation.

Exodus Chapter 31, verse 12: *And the Lord spoke to Moses saying Speak thou also unto the children of Israel saying, "verily my Sabbaths ye shall keep for it is a sign between me and you throughout your generations; that ye may know that I am the Lord that doth sanctify you.*

Verse 17: *"It is a sign between me and the children of Israel for ever for in six days the Lord made heaven and* *earth, and on **the seventh day He rested and was refreshed**".*

Matthew 11, verse 27: *"And all things are delivered unto me of my Father and no man knoweth the Son, but the Father; neither knoweth any man the Father, save the Son, and he to whomsoever the Son will reveal him. Come unto me all ye that labour and are heavy laden and I will give you rest. Take my yoke upon you and learn of me; for I am meek and lowly in heart: and ye shall find rest unto your souls, for my yoke is easy and my burden is light."*

Heaven is a place of work and Heaven is a place of rest, in the same way earth is a place of work and a place of rest.

Hebrews Chapter 3, verse 7: *"Wherefore (as the Holy Ghost saith, today if you will hear his voice, harden not your hearts, as in the provocation in the day of temptation in the wilderness, when your fathers tempted me, proved me, and saw my works forty years. Wherefore I was grieved with that generation, and said, they do always err in their heart; and they have not known my ways. So I sware in my wrath that they shall not enter into my rest"*

Hebrews 3, Verses 16-19: *"For who, having heard, rebelled? Indeed, was it not all who came out of Egypt, led by Moses? 17 Now with whom was He angry forty years? Was it not with those who sinned, whose corpses fell in the wilderness? 18 And to whom did He swear that they would not enter His rest, but to those who did not obey? 19 So we see that they could not enter in because of unbelief".*

Hebrews Chapter 4:1-10: *"Therefore, since a promise remains of entering His rest, let us fear lest any of you seem to have come short of it. 2 For indeed the gospel was preached to us as well as to them; but the word which they heard did not profit them,[a] not being mixed with faith in those who heard it. 3 For we who have believed do enter that rest, as He has said: " So I swore in My wrath, ' They shall not enter My rest,' although the works were finished from the foundation of the world. 4 For He has spoken in a certain place of the seventh day in this way: "And God rested on the seventh day from all His works"; 5 and again in this place: "They shall not enter My rest." 6 Since therefore it remains that some must enter it, and those to whom it was first preached did not enter because of disobedience, 7 again He designates a certain day, saying in David, "Today," after such a long time, as it has been said: " Today, if you will hear His voice, Do not harden your hearts." 8 For if Joshua* *had given them rest, then He would not afterward have spoken of another day. 9 There remains therefore a rest for the people of God. 10 For he who has entered His rest has himself also ceased from his works as God did from His".*

Rest is a slice of heaven that makes you know the work has been done. After God had done everything, He rested and was refreshed. You here on earth interacting with Heaven, after you have seen that this situation has been settled in heaven, you here on earth then enter into His rest, so that here on earth you are no longer moved by what you see, because you have seen the end result already. For example, if Chelsea and Arsenal want to play and God takes you to heaven to watch the match before it begins, so you have seen that Arsenal won 10 - 0. If you are an Arsenal fan and God has shown you that and the match starts and it appears as if Chelsea are playing brilliantly and Arsenal playing in a poor manner you will be at rest, because you know the end result. This is how we are supposed to react to situations on earth. We are not supposed to run all over the place like headless chickens not knowing what is going on.

You are supposed to understand that he that has entered His rest has ceased from his own work. God only rested when the work was complete and finished. God does not begin what He has not already finished. So what looks like a beginning to you, God has already seen the end of it. To you it's a beginning; you don't know what will happen tomorrow. To God He has seen not only tomorrow, but also next century. Therefore, when you are here on earth and confronted with situations; and you tap into the interactions between heaven and earth, you catch a glimpse of heaven, you then enter His rest based on what you receive in heaven and suddenly nothing on earth seems to perturb you anymore.

People will be wondering why you are not worried any more, everyone is worried and crying and you are just cool because you have seen what they have not seen. That is interaction between heaven and earth. **When you see heaven and heaven has spoken you enter rest here on earth.** You cannot access the rest of heavens blessings until you enter into His rest.

Do you refresh others or are you a pressure cooker? **Ability to enter rest on earth is dependent on your ability to access heaven from earth.** Once you access heaven from earth over a situation you enter a rest in your heart about that situation. In Philemon chapter 1; Philemon refreshed others.

In 2 Timothy Chapter 1, Verse 15-18; Paul was refreshed by others. If your body will not rest, then your soul will rest in peace. Understand therefore that you should not work yourself to death physically. *"The blessings of God maketh rich and adds no sorrow to it"*. It's not about holding down 10 jobs, or doing all overtime available, that is not what makes you rich, ask God to give you rest in your spirit, soul and body. Heaven is a place of work and Heaven is a place of rest, so also is earth. Access heaven so that you can enter into His rest here on earth.

God worked and God rested, **we however, can only enter into His rest, if we have access to heaven while we are still here on earth.** Enter into the rest of God today; this is the benefit of interaction between heaven and earth. It is time for you to begin to live on earth with heavens privileges.

*"Come to Me, all you who labour and are heavy laden, and **I will give you rest**. Take My yoke upon you and learn from Me, for I am gentle and lowly in heart, and you will find rest for your souls. For My yoke is easy and My burden is light."* Matthew 11:28-30.

*"So there is a full **complete rest** still waiting for the people of God."* Hebrews 4:9 (LB).

Jesus promised us rest for our souls when we came, accepted Him and learned of Him. Hebrews tells us, we receive a full rest, for those who believe wholly and completely on Jesus. When we are born again we enter into God's rest positionally. We then need to enjoy same by progressionally entering God's rest through knowledge of the Word and interaction between heaven and earth.

Webster's Dictionary defines rest as - ***being at peace or ease.*** Isn't that wonderful? We as believers can be at peace and ease in Christ. No matter what you are

Chapter 6: Entering into God's Rest

going through, you can be at peace or ease, because as a believer, you have entered into God's rest. But do you know that? Have you embraced this fact?

"Then all this assembly shall know that the Lord does not save with sword and spear; for the battle is the Lord's, and He will give you into our hands." 1 Samuel 17:47.

"And he said, "Listen, all you of Judah and you inhabitants of Jerusalem, and you, King Jehoshaphat! Thus says the Lord to you: `Do not be afraid nor dismayed because of this great multitude, for the battle is not yours, but God's." 2 Chronicles 20:15.

When we are born again, God wants us to enter in and dwell in His rest. He wants to fight our battles for us! In fact, when you really consider the work wrought by Jesus on the cross, the battle is already won! (Colossians 2:15).

Jesus defeated Satan in Hell, arose victorious over our adversary the devil. Satan is a defeated foe, and anything He throws at you is really a lost cause, if you will dwell in God's rest. How do I do that? **You have**

to take the giant step of completely trusting in, and relying on God. You have to totally accept what Jesus did on the cross, what He accomplished for you and act like God's Word is true!

Actions do speak louder than words. In the case of a believer, both our words and actions are important. We must act like and talk like the Word of God is true. Such audacity comes easily to those with connection to heaven while on earth. This is the basis of dominion living.

OUR SUFFICIENCY IN HEAVEN

*Blessed be the God and Father of our Lord Jesus Christ, who **has blessed us with every spiritual blessing in the heavenly places** in Christ, just as He chose us in Him before the foundation of the world, that we should be holy and without blame before Him in love, having predestined us to adoption as sons by Jesus Christ to Himself, according to the good pleasure of His will".* Ephesians 1:3-5

The bible says God has blessed us with every spiritual blessing in heavenly places. Why are the blessings in heavenly places? Why not on earth? Is that not what many of us are looking for? But he has blessed us with heavenly blessings in heaven even though he knows we are operating on earth.

Now that we have established the need to interact with heaven while still in earth; Let us look at believers sufficiency and reserve in heaven; i.e., how to open a heaven's bank account. How do you spend from God's pocket?

It's like me saying I know you live in the United Kingdom, but I have blessed you with every blessing in Russia. How does that help you in the United Kingdom. He has blessed us with every blessing in **heavenly places,** which means there must be interaction between heaven places and earth for us to be able to activate and access those blessings. Otherwise God could have put those blessings all on earth; but he said he has blessed us with all the blessings in heavenly places. Heavenly places is a spirit dimension that is heaven but which are expected to be able to access from the earth.

Why every blessing in heavenly places? Why did God put those blessings in heavenly places even though the

Chapter 7: Our Sufficiency in Heaven

recipients of it are here on earth? Let's look at the believers reserve in heaven.

Practically all countries in the world have a **foreign reserve** i.e., a form of asset that a country holds in liquid cash externally to its national financial operations. These are assets of the a nation's central bank held in different reserve currencies, mostly the US dollar, and to a lesser extent the euro, the UK pound, and the Japanese yen, and used to back its liabilities, e.g. the local currency issued, and the various bank reserves deposited with the central bank, by the government or financial institutions.

> *We are living on earth, but the spiritual blessings are not stored where we live; otherwise anybody can get to it easily.*

So that regardless of what happens within the local economy, the country's external financial buying power is not affected. This means regardless of what happens to the national currency; a $50 billion dollars foreign reserve remains $50 billion dollars. The nation's ability to buy externally is not affected. The foreign reserve is held out of harm's way so to speak. The money is shielded from local activities. It can of course be drawn upon from time to time to meet local domestic needs.

Similarly God has kept a foreign reserve for His children. This is why He has blessed us with every spiritual blessing, but has kept it in heavenly places. **Our citizenship is in heaven so we are strangers in a strange land on earth.** We are God's ambassadors.

*"Dear friends, I warn you as **"temporary residents and foreigners"** to keep away from **worldly desires** that wage war against your very souls. [12] Be careful to live properly among your unbelieving neighbours. Then even if they accuse you of doing wrong, they will see your honourable behaviour, and they will give honour to God when he judges the world".* 1 Pet.2:11-12. (NLT)

If you go to the American Embassy in Somalia it still looks great and like a fortress (compared to other embassies); this is because the embassy is always a reflection of the wealth and strength of America and not a reflection of the poverty and depravation in Somalia. The ability of American Ambassador in Somalia to live well is not a product of what is happening in Somalia; but a reflection of what America can afford. So what is happening in the home country (America) is the most important factor to the Ambassador's quality of live in Somalia.

God has blessed us with every spiritual blessing (which is needed to translate to physical blessing), but the blessing is stashed away in heavenly places; therefore our ability to live on should not be dependent on what is happening where we live (on earth), but on the condition of our home country (heaven), from where we have been sent. Our inability to interact with heavenly places has been limiting us; hence whenever the earth shuts the door we reach our own limitation as well. Now you can see that if we indeed need to die before accessing heavenly places (as some wrongly believes); then we are in big trouble. Why will God keep our spiritual blessing needed to live in dominion on earth in a place we cannot access from the earth? That will not be fair will it?

All the ambassador has to do is call the State/Foreign department at home and they will send whatever he wants with the diplomatic bag, which cannot be searched. They can bring in whatever they like and stock their embassy regardless of what is happening in the wider local community. God has blessed us with every spiritual blessing but this is not kept on earth even though the beneficiaries are on earth.

If you lay up treasures for yourself on earth corruption etc., can get to it. We are living on earth, but the spiritual blessings are not where we live. Now you can see the foolishness of those who feel we need to die to experience heaven. Because if God has blessed us with every spiritual blessing in heavenly places and we don't interact with heaven from the earth, how will we access it? If we have to wait till we die then we are in trouble because we will not be able to access what God has blessed us with. The blessings have been kept in heavenly places.

God kept our spiritual blessing in heavenly places where moth and corruption cannot touch it, ready for deployment to earth as and when requested. Do you know that every American Embassy in the world has a secure form of communication to Washington; both voice and data? That is the way the Ambassador briefs his bosses back in the US as to what is going on and also passes on intelligence.

> *Our inability to interact with heavenly places has been limiting us; hence whenever the earth shuts the door we reach our own limitation as well.*

Also, unless the home country knows what is going on they won't send any supplies to the ambassador. So it behoves the ambassador to make requests to the home country of whatever it is he needs. In the same way, even though we have been blessed with every spiritual blessing in heavenly places, it just does not jump at us unless we call for it. And that calling, is what we sometimes call prayer, declaration and sometimes confession.

So our prayer is what I call earthly licence for heaven intervention. We know this exists in the spirit and we are calling heaven to say we need say bread in abundant supply. This way we can live the days of heaven on earth regardless of the economic situations on earth. This is the secret of living above the world's economic system. This is how we can live above the attacks of Babylon.

Matthew 6 in verse 19 the bible says *"do not lay up for yourself treasure on earth, where moth and rust destroy and where thieves break in and steal. But* **lay up for yourself treasures in heaven**, *where neither moth nor rust destroys and where thieves do not break in and steal.*

God said I am going to have a family on earth but I will keep the resources where no corruption can touch it. Because I expect that family on earth to maintain contact and an interaction with the home base so that whatever they need, I can then supply. But at the least I will know that the material is in a place that is secure.

Blessed are your eyes for reading this book. This realisation will make you fearless, regardless of what is happening around you or in the economy you operate in. Since you understand your citizenship is in heaven; you can be assured of uninterrupted supply regardless of the famine in your land.

1 Peter Chapter 1, verse 3: *"Blessed be the God the father of our Lord Jesus Christ who according to His abundant mercy has begotten us again to a living hope through the resurrection of His Son, Jesus Christ from the dead to an **inheritance incorruptible** and undefiled that does not fade away reserved <u>in heaven</u> for you"*.

Scripture is interpreting scriptures here. God has given you an **inheritance incorruptible and undefiled** because it is not on earth, if it was on earth all those things would come upon it. This means there is no shortage, and anyone can download what they need from heaven without affecting your downloads, because yours is already reserved. There is nothing like somebody asking for too much from heaven. Your own portion has been reserved for you. **The purpose of heaven's reserve is so that God can pay for everything He orders here on earth.** That is why when God instructs you, He is not bothered about the resources you need to fulfil that instruction because He knows He already has a reserve. Our job is to obey God and leave the consequences to Him.

The foreign reserve of any country is always an added extra to their domestic budget. It's an add on. The domestic budget excludes the foreign reserve. It is not something you use for every domestic activity. We are supposed to live naturally supernaturally and supernaturally naturally. For instance, when they came to Jesus for taxes and the money was not there; Jesus said "no problem" let me now call on my foreign reserve. *Peter, you are a fisherman, go down to the water and the first fish you catch, open its mouth and get the money.* Peter opened the mouth of the fish and found a gold coin there.

Fish don't have money in their mouth. But when your foreign reserve wants to release blessing, anything can happen. Jesus did not go round opening the mouth of every single fish every day collecting money; but He demonstrated that we are here on earth to interact with heaven and whenever we encounter any limitation here on earth, call on your foreign reserve and your foreign reserve will manifest on earth and your limitation is removed. You can therefore see that Jesus demonstrated the principle.

"When they had come to Capernaum, those who received the temple tax came to Peter and said, "Does your Teacher not pay the temple tax?" He said, "Yes." And when he had come into the house, Jesus anticipated him, saying, "What do you think, Simon? From whom do the kings of the earth take customs or taxes, from their sons or from strangers?" Peter said to Him, "From strangers." Jesus said to him, "Then the sons are free. Nevertheless, lest we offend them, go to the sea, cast in a hook, and take the fish that comes up first. And when you have opened its mouth, you will find a piece of money; take that and give it to them for Me and you." Mat 17:24-27

> When God instructs, He is not bothered about the resources you need to fulfil that instruction. Our job is to obey God and leave the consequences to Him.

Jesus did not pick money from the mouth of the fish as a normal day to day activity, just like your foreign reserve is not what you spend on your every day domestic activity. It was just to show you that there is no limit or restriction to you here on earth, your only restriction is your faith.

The reason I am trying to make this very clear is that some people may think having a foreign reserve means they should not work on earth, this is not the case. This does not mean you should not interact with the earth at all. God expects us to work hard and be diligent. The purpose of the heavenly foreign reserve is not for you to stop earthly work, and sit at home and draw on your foreign reserve – it does not work like that. However, if you go to work and earn £1,000 per month and then have a genuine sudden extra expense of £2,000 at the end of the month, that is when you may draw on your heavenly reserve to make up the difference; it means there is no limitation to you. Favour and mercy are still God's favourite languages.

Don't allow your earthly situation to limit you. You have cast iron diplomatic immunity from earthly limitations and encumbrances. When the bible says "seek ye first the kingdom of God...." It says "your father knows you have need of these things". How? He has already created a reserve reserved for you in heaven. Your foreign reserve is what distinguishes you from the heathen here on earth. They hit a roadblock and don't know where to go, but you can draw on your foreign reserve. They start to wonder what has happened; after all you work in the same place and are confronted with the same limitations. However, your own story is different. That is a testimony of every child of God.

We are quick to accept the words of society. Many doctors don't know their left from their right; when it comes to certain ailments. For every expert who says one thing, you will find others saying the exact opposite. If care is not taken you will allow your life to be lived in constant alarm and you won't know what to do. You have to be still and trust God. Experts have their limitations. Too many people have cancer and the doctor has given them six months to live and twenty years later, they are still alive. Doctors are not God, they have an opinion based on their limited knowledge. And that's why the bible says *"whose report will you believe?"* The report you believe will determine your outcome. I choose to believe the report of the Lord. It's important for you to understand that it does not matter how disadvantaged you think you are; you can still access your reserve in heaven.

Do you know that most of the people God used in the bible, from Abraham to the days of Jesus are the so called "rejects" of society, murderers, fornicators, adulterers, idol worshippers? These are the people God used to prove the point, that it is not who you are that matters it is who you become in Christ that matters. It's very important that you don't despise yourself and think you are disadvantage, I am a black man, or I don't have a degree. I am from a poor home. I asked someone recently "what school did Joseph go to, who was his pastor? How many degrees did he have? Nothing. Did that stop him from becoming the Prime Minister of Egypt? When the hand of the Lord is upon you, nothing else matters. The purpose of heaven's reserve is so that God can pay for everything He orders on earth.

Phillipians Chapter 3. Verse 20. *For **our citizenship is in heaven** from which we also eagerly wait for the Saviour, the Lord Jesus Christ, who will transform our lowly body* *that it may be conformed to his glorious body according to the working by which He is able even to subdue all things to himself.*

Our citizenship is in heaven; hence we have access to heaven's reserve to pay for things here on earth. God's man, doing God's work, in God's way at God's time, will never lack God's resources. Let this be clear, God pays for what He orders and not what you have added yourself. That is extra. Those who are alive and awake to this reality of heaven's reserve live differently on earth. To live a life of financial dominion on earth is to use the resources exclusively available in heaven to overcome the limitations imposed on earth.

Those who know how to connect heaven and download information needed for missions on earth will never bow to gold or mammon. Let us examine some examples of those whose heaven's reserve became a revelation to them and immediately changed their attitude to things happening here on earth.

Abraham: On his way back from the battle of the Kings, he met Melchizedek, who triggered something in him. Genesis 14.

"And he brought back all the goods and also brought back his kinsman Lot and his possessions, the women also and the people. After his [Abram's] return from the defeat and slaying of Chedorlaomer and the kings who were with him, the king of Sodom went out to meet him at the Valley of Shaveh, that is, the King's Valley. Melchizedek king of Salem [later called Jerusalem] brought out bread and wine [for their nourishment]; he was the priest of God Most High, And he blessed him and said, **Blessed (favoured with blessings, made blissful, joyful) be Abram by God Most High, Possessor and Maker of heaven and earth**, *And blessed, praised, and glorified be God Most High, Who has given your foes into your hand! And [Abram] gave him a tenth of all [he had taken]. And the king of Sodom said to Abram, Give me the persons and keep the goods for yourself. But Abram said to the king of Sodom, I have lifted up my hand and sworn to the Lord, God Most High,* **the Possessor and Maker of heaven and earth**, *That I would not take a thread or a shoelace or anything that is yours, lest you should say, I have made Abram rich.*
[Take all] except only what my young men have eaten and the share of the men [allies] who went with me--Aner, Eshcol, and Mamre; let them take their portion.
Genesis14:16-24 (AMP)

Based on the words of Melchizedek Abram's response was *"I have lifted up my hands unto God the most high, <u>the possessor of heaven and earth</u> that I will not take anything from you lest you should say I have made Abraham rich."* What Melchizedek said triggered something in Abram.

He turned down the earthly offer as good as it was because he now realised he had reserves in heaven. He served a God that is the possessor of heaven and earth. It's not natural for a man to turn those things away but he did so because he saw something better. Later on, the Lord blessed Abraham in all things.

> *When it comes to God anything can be suspended here on earth, the spiritual can overrule the natural*

"Jesus answered, "If I honour Myself, My honour is nothing. It is My Father who honours Me, of whom you say that He is your God. ⁵⁵ Yet you have not known Him, but I know Him. And if I say, 'I do not know Him,' I shall be a liar like you; but I do know Him and keep His word. ⁵⁶ Your *father **Abraham rejoiced to see My day, and he saw it and was glad.**"* John 8:54-56

Abraham saw something that compelled him to go with God's way of doing things.

Daniel: The King promised a world to anyone who could interpret the handwriting on the wall; Daniel demonstrated that he spent from Heavens reserve. The king had a most generous offer for anyone who could interpret the writing.

Even though we are in the world we are not of the world. We have a reserve in heaven. There is no scarcity in the kingdom of God. Because of our knowledge of our heaven's reserve we know we can live recession-free even though there is a recession

Daniel Chapter 5 verse 17-20: *then Daniel answered and said before the king, let your gifts be to thyself, and give thy rewards to another; yet I will read the writing unto the king and make known to him the interpretation". Oh King, the most High God gave Nebuchadnezar thy father a kingdom and majesty and glory and honour; and for the majesty that* *he gave him, all people, nations, and languages, trembled and feared before him: whom he would he slew; and whom he would he kept alive; and whom he would he set up; and whom he would he put down. But when his heart was lifted up and his mind hardened in pride, he was deposed from his kingly thone, and they took his glory from him.*

Here you can see that for Daniel to reject the king's generous offer he must have other resources they did not know of. To put this in perspective, we have to remember these people were in captivity and the reward could have set him up for life physically, but he rejected it; this was because he had seen something spiritually that allowed him to say no to a physical reward. It's important for you to understand that what happens on earth does not matter once you understand what you have access to in heaven. We have an inheritance which the lord has reserved for us in heaven and we have access to those things here on earth as and when needed to perpetuate Gods vision for our lives

Nehemiah: In Nehemiah Chapter 2. Verse 19 after Nehemiah was confronted and challenged what did he do? This is just to strengthen the case.

"But when Sanbalat the Horonite and Tobiah the servant, the Ammonite and Geshem the Arabian heard it, they laughed us to scorn and despised us and said what is this thing that ye do? Will ye rebel against the king?" Then answered I them, and said unto them, "The God of heaven, ***He will prosper us; therefore we his servants will arise and build;*** *but ye have no portion, nor right, nor memorial in Jerusalem".*

Everything was stacked up against him but it did not matter because he knew he had his reserve where no one could touch it.

I hope a few things have now been established in your heart:
1. God has blessed you with all spiritual blessing in heavenly places.
2. You have an inheritance which the lord has reserved for you in heavenly places.

So, how do you open heaven's bank account? There **are three dimensions to our heaven's reserve**. We have indescribable and undefiled reserves in heaven.

And we have been taught that the only way to access it is by sowing and reaping. This is not wrong, but is simply the **first dimension**.

Sowing and reaping is not all there is to heaven's abundance and we need to go further. In the wilderness, the children of Israel did not sow any seed and yet they were provided for, this proves there are other dimensions to God's provision.

In Genesis the bible talks about sowing and reaping as long as earth remains. In other words, sowing and reaping and seed time and harvest time relates to the earth, but our citizenship is in heaven. The other dimensions are not earthly based. **You have to walk in the first dimension before getting to the other dimensions.** Don't leave here thinking sowing and reaping is nullified. That is not the case, however you have to walk in the first dimension before you get to the others. God was a cloud by day and a pillar of fire by night for the children of Israel. When you live the days of heaven on earth the normal weather patterns do not apply.

When it comes to God anything can be suspended here on earth, the spiritual can overrule the natural, don't limit yourself to physical things. The **second dimension** enables us to access heavenly reserves and is called **Inheritance – reaping where you have not necessarily sown.**

John Chapter 4, from verse 35. *"Do you not say there are still four months and then comes the harvest behold I say unto you lift up your eyes and look on the fields; for they are white already to harvest"*, *and he who reaps receives wages and gathers fruit for eternal life that both he who sows and he who reaps may rejoice together for in this the saying is true. And herein the saying is true, one sows and another reaps.* **I sent you to reap <u>that for which you have not laboured</u>. Others have laboured and you have entered into their labours."**

> *When the sin age comes to an end in your life; you are a walking miracle everywhere you go.*

This means you are reaping where you have not sown. This does not mean we should stop sowing, it simply

Chapter 7: Our Sufficiency in Heaven

means there is a second dimension of harvest, which is your inheritance. **These are things that are yours because of whose you are and because of in whom you are.** For example, if I come to your house and give your children £100.00 each; they are getting it simply because of my relationship with their parents, thus they are reaping where they have not sown, they are reaping because of whose children they are. There are things that will come into your life simply because you are a child of God.

First dimension is where you reap and sow and the second dimension is where God just looks at you and blesses you because of whose you are. We need to lift ourselves above the first dimension. Inheritance is accessed only through who you are and whose you are. It is all about the depth of your relationship with God. It's all about your connection with God. There are things that God will bring your way simply because He is pleased with you.

The **third dimension of harvest** is the **end of the age**. Matthew 13 from verse 36. *"Then Jesus sent the multitude away and went into the house and his disciples* *came unto him saying explain to us the parable of tares of the field, he answered and said to them, he who sows the good seed is the son of man, the field is the world the good seed are the sons of the kingdom but the tares are the sons of the wicked one, the enemy who sowed them is the devil, **the harvest is the end of the age**; and the reapers are the angels.*

This is the bull's eye; the third dimension of harvest is the end of age. Sin is the root cause of shortage, for all have sinned and fallen short of the glory of God. If the third dimension of harvest is end of the age, it means you **enter a dimension where you can perpetually draw from heavens account and resources when the sin age comes to an end in your life.** You will never know shortage again in your life.

When the sin age comes to an end in your life, you are a walking miracle everywhere you go. This is where holiness meets prosperity. Lack will no longer exists in your dictionary.

John 17 from verse 6: *"I have manifested your name to the men you have given Me, out of the world, they are yours, you gave them to me and they have kept your word, now they have known that all things which you have given me are from you for I have given to them the words which you gave me and they have received them and have known surely that I came forth from you have believed that you sent me. I pray for them, I pray not for the world, but for them which thou has given me for they are thine. And all mine are yours and all yours are mine and I am glorified in them".*

This is not just about tithes and offering. All means all. **All of God is yours when all of your is His.** And as long as sin is in our lives, "all of us" is not yet God's. Because He is not yet 100% in control. **But when the sin age comes to an end in our lives and all of our life becomes God's then all of God's becomes ours.**

How can you have unhindered access to heaven's reserves? You can only have unhindered access by opening a bank account in heaven. To open an account here on earth, you need identification and sign some documents and the bank will then give you your account number and card through which you can access the account contents.

HOW TO OPEN A RESERVE ACCOUNT IN HEAVEN

Philippians Chapter 4. From Verse 10. *"But I rejoiced in the Lord greatly, for now at last your care of me hath flourished greatly again wherein you were also careful but also lacked opportunity. Not that I speak in regard to need, but I have learned in whatever state I am to be content, I have learned both to be abased and abound everywhere and in all things I have learned to be full and to be hungry both to abound and to suffer need. I can do all things through Christ who strengthens me. Nevertheless you have done well in that you shared in my distress, now you Phillipians know also that in the beginning of the gospel, when I departed from Macedonia, no church communicated with me as concerning giving and receiving but ye only. For even in Thessalonica you sent once and again to my necessity. Not because I desire a gift; but I desire fruit that may abound **to your account".**

Opening an account in heaven is not just a cliché. The account referred to here is not a physical account, it is the account in heavenly places, in verse 18 it says *"indeed I have all and abound, I am full, having received from Epaphroditus the things which were sent from you, an odour of a sweet smell, a sacrifice, acceptable, well pleasing to God and my God shall supply all your need according to His riches in Glory by Christ Jesus".*

To open an account with God in heaven does not begin with tithes and offering. **It begins with you SETTING YOUR AFFECTIONS ON THINGS ABOVE.**

Colossians 3 verse 1. *"If ye then be risen with Christ, seek those things which are above, where Christ sitteth on the right hand of God. Set your affection on things above, not on things on the earth. For ye are dead, and your life is hid with Christ in God".*

You have to love God passionately and walk in the circle of love to begin the process of opening a bank account in heaven. You have to set your affection on the things above. You have to give God all your heart first before you give him your hand or resources.

Colossians 3:1 is convicting, encouraging, and challenging to believers. It is an exhortation to live in a completely different way than the people of the world. It is a call to have different goals, thoughts, and passions — a completely different worldview. This text calls us to direct our minds out of the temporary, the sin, corruption, pain, death, and evil of this world and to focus our thoughts on eternal life, who we will be with, and what we will be doing for all eternity. In the first two chapters of Colossians, Paul addresses the supremacy of Christ and in the last two chapters he addresses how believers are to walk because of Christ's supremacy. You need to know who you are in Christ.

Paul goes on to say, *"Set your mind on the things above, not on the things that are on earth."* The first command is to desire, long for, and seek heavenly things; this command is to mentally dwell on the things above. God wants you to fix, set, and cement into place your mind so that it is directed to think about heaven not earthly things. You have to be focused on things above to be able to tune to heaven's frequency.

It doesn't matter how old you are, life is short compare to eternity and Christ could take you home to be with Him when He wants. God doesn't want your mind thinking about sin, about things destined to perish, about the world's goods that will be burnt up, but he wants you to set or fix your mind on the things above.

The command is clear; **Set your hearts on things above where Christ is.** Set your minds on things above, not on earthly things. In other words, look up. C.S. Lewis said, *"if you read history, you will find that the Christians who did most for the present world were just those who thought most of the next. The Apostles themselves, who set on foot the conversion of the Roman Empire, the great men who built up the Middle Ages, the English Evangelicals who abolished the Slave Trade, all left their mark on Earth, precisely because their minds were occupied with Heaven"* (The Joyful Christian, p.138). In other words, to be of earthly good, maintain a heavenly focus. Look up.

Next time you find your mind wandering and thinking about worldly or sinful things, stop yourself and start thinking about heavenly things. Picture in your mind what cherubim and seraphim look like. Think about what it will be like to talk to Noah, Abraham, Joseph, Moses and any other saint you can think of. Think about what it will be like to walk on streets of gold, what you will look like, what others will look like in their glorified states.

Think about what it will be like to talk to Jesus Christ, to ask Him questions about His life, His works, why

He chose to save you. Read the portions of Scripture that speak of Heaven and set your mind working to ponder, meditate, and imagine what it will be like to be given a glorified body, to live in a perfect world with no sin, where you can learn with a perfect mind, and remember with a perfect memory for all eternity. Set your mind on the things above! Let heaven be your model and standard.

*"All these died in faith, without receiving the promises, but having seen them and welcomed them from a distance, and **having confessed that they were strangers and exiles on the earth.** For those who say such things make it clear that they are seeking a country of their own. And indeed if they had been thinking of that country from which they went out, they would have had opportunity to return. But as it is, they desire a better country, that is a heavenly one. Therefore God is not ashamed to be called their God; for He has prepared a city for them."* Heb 11:13-16

These Old Testament believers, although less informed than we are of God's purposes, set their hearts on His eternal plans. The effect was that they lived with the knowledge that they were no more than visitors to a foreign country. We are told that if they had desired to return to their homeland, then they would have been able to. Abraham, like all the others listed, rejected that option, being confident in THE LORD's promises and so kept his eyes on eternity. What a guy! What a Faith. What a Trust.

So this is about being fully functional on earth, but having a direct line with heaven daily. This is not about over-spiritualisation, as some may be tempted. **It is about confronting the daily issues of life in the marketplace with heaven's wisdom and directions.** We have already seen the abject failure of reliance on natural and intellectual knowledge alone.

Matthew 16: 23 : *"but He turned and said to Peter, get behind me satan for your are a stumbling block unto me. For thou mindest not the things of God but the things of man".*

Another translation puts it this way: *But he turning to Peter said "get out of my way Satan. You are a danger to me because your mind is not on the things of God but on the things of the earth".*

How can you be a danger to Christ? When your mind is not on the things of God but on the things of man. If your heart is not set on the things of God, then you are a danger to Him and He will not give you the secret code to his account. It is very important that you understand this.

HEAVEN'S ACCOUNT NUMBER

My symbolic Heaven Account Number is: **COC2COR899815**
[COC (Charles Omole Clan). 2 Cor 8:9; 9:8 and 15]
"For ye know that grace of our Lord Jesus Christ, that though He was rich, yet for your sakes he became poor, that ye through his poverty might be rich". 2 Cor 8:9

"And God is able to make all grace abound toward you that ye always having all sufficiency in all things, may abound to all good work" 2Cor 9:8

"Thanks be to God for His indescribable Grace". 2Cor 9:15

So this account number relates to me and my seed and their generation. It starts with acceptance of the **divine exchange** that has happened in Christ Jesus. Then I believe that I will manifest all sufficiency in all things; without exception. I then maintain and water what God has done with Praise and thanksgiving. **These are the key ingredients of a heaven's account.** You can write your own account number in the same way. God is no respecter of persons.

> *The problem with many of us is that we tend to see only limitations. We don't understand that we have reserves in heaven*

Because of his divine grace, which gives me access, I now have all sufficiency in all things. Heavens bank account means there is no limitation to my withdrawals. You cannot run an account you have not yet opened. Tithes and offering are ways of running an account. But the account must be opened first; by setting our affections on the things above.

The problem with many of us is that we tend to see only limitations. We don't understand that we have reserves in heaven we can call on to overrule the earthly limitations we face. As a result we have been living a paradox; the scriptures says that *"the slaves are riding horses and the princes are walking on foot"*. The people who are supposed to be riding horses are now the ones walking and everything is now upside down because we are not exercising our authority.

Your story must change in Jesus name. I prophesy increase over your life. The Lord will exalt your horn like the horn of a unicorn. He will anoint your head with fresh oil. He will give you a fresh enablement from on high to make you fit for His purpose. It is your season to shine. Be bold, be strong; for the Lord your God is with you.

You can live a life of dominion on earth, by connecting with heaven. All limits are removed from your path from this moment in the name of Jesus. You are blessed beyond terror. Let us all walk in the reality of the revelation in this book and take over the marketplace for Christ. God bless you.

THE EPILOGUE

The Domain of the King
Understanding your Destiny of Dominion in the Kingdom of God

Now that we have established the reality of interactions between heaven and earth; I will like us to end this journey by looking at the manner in which we are supposed to now live on earth as citizens of heaven. How do we live in Dominion on earth as citizens of heaven? Yes we need to maintain a permanent connection with home-base (Heaven); but how do we outwardly exercise dominion on earth at the same time.

The earth is a domain of heaven; that is why interaction is possible between heaven and earth. Living the days of heaven on earth; involves us exercising dominion over the domain/kingdom called earth. It is now all about the Kingdom.

Understanding Dominion

"²⁶Then God said, "Let Us make man in Our image, according to Our likeness; let them have dominion over the fish of the sea, over the birds of the air, and over the cattle, over all[] the earth and over every creeping thing that creeps on the earth." ²⁷So God created man in His own image; in the image of God He created him; male and female He created them. ²⁸Then God blessed them, and God said to them, "Be fruitful and multiply<u>; fill the earth and subdue it; have dominion over</u> the fish of the sea, over the birds of the air, and over every living thing that moves on the earth." **Genesis 1:26-28**

God created man to have dominion. Dominion speaks of Kingdom or domain. Man lost it at Eden, but in Christ, the Dominion or Rulership of the Kingdom is restored back to man.

"Until John the Baptist began to preach, the laws of Moses and the messages of the prophets were your guides. <u>But now the Good News of the Kingdom of God is preached</u>, and eager multitudes are forcing their way in. ¹⁷But that doesn't mean that the law has lost its force in even the smallest point. It is stronger and more permanent than heaven and earth. **Luke 16 [NLT]**

Epilogue

Up until John the Baptist, the Law of Moses was fully operational. The people also had the books of the prophets (all announcing the coming of the King, the Messiah). The first five books of the Bible are known as the "Pentateuch" or the "Books of Moses" these are;

<u>Genesis</u> – Creation, the fall, sin, how Israel came to be a nation and then came to be in Egypt.

<u>Exodus</u> – The deliverance of the people of Israel from slavery in Egypt.

<u>Leviticus</u> – The book of the law.

<u>Numbers</u> – The wandering in the wilderness.

<u>Deuteronomy</u> – Israel preparing to move into the Promised Land.

After the books of the Law (the first 5 books of the bible), From Joshua to Malachi are the books of the prophetic writings). They all spoke about Jesus. The master confirms this himself on the Road to Emmaus:

Luke 24:13-27 - *[13] Now behold, two of them were travelling that same day to a village called Emmaus, which was seven miles[1] from Jerusalem. [14]And they talked together of all these things which had happened. [15]So it was, while they conversed and reasoned, that Jesus Himself drew near and went with them. [16]But their eyes were restrained, so that they did not know Him.*

[17]And He said to them, "What kind of conversation is this that you have with one another as you walk and are sad?"[2] [18]Then the one whose name was Cleopas answered and said to Him, "Are You the only stranger in Jerusalem, and have You not known the things which happened there in these days?"

[19]And He said to them, "What things?" So they said to Him, "The things concerning Jesus of Nazareth, who was a Prophet mighty in deed and word before God and all the people, [20]and how the chief priests and our rulers delivered Him to be condemned to death, and crucified Him. [21]But we were hoping that it was He who was going to redeem Israel. Indeed, besides all this, today is the third day since these things happened.

[22]Yes, and certain women of our company, who arrived at the tomb early, astonished us. [23]When they did not find His body, they came saying that they had also seen a vision of angels who said He was alive.

24And certain of those who were with us went to the tomb and found it just as the women had said; but Him they did not see." 25Then He said to them, "O foolish ones, and slow of heart to believe in all that the prophets have spoken! 26Ought not the Christ to have suffered these things and to enter into His glory?" <u>27And beginning at Moses and all the Prophets, He expounded to them in all the Scriptures the things concerning Himself.</u>

Christ is the theme of the entire revelation of God's word. He is promised in Genesis, revealed in the law, prefigured in its history, praised in its poetry, proclaimed in its prophecy provided in its Gospels, proved in its Acts, pre-eminent in its Epistles and prevailing in Revelation.

He is seen in every verse and every book of the Bible. In many types and shadows Christ was revealed in the Old Testament. In all cases; **more than one representations of Him exist in each book**; but we let's take a look at **a typical depiction of Christ** in the Bible. It's a matter of personal revelation.

Take a journey through the halls of the Bible and in every one of them you will see Christ.

JESUS IN ALL SCRIPTURES

1. In **Genesis**, He is the **promised Seed**
2. In **Exodus**, He is the **Smitten Rock**
3. In **Leviticus,** He is the **sacrificial Lamb**
4. In **Numbers,** He is the **Brazen Serpent**
5. In **Deuteronomy**, He is the **Prophet like unto Moses**
6. In **Joshua**, He is **Captain of the Lord's hosts**
7. In **Judges**, He is the **Messenger of Jehovah**
8. In **Ruth**, He is the **Kinsman Redeemer**
9. In **1 Samuel**, He is **the Great Judge**
10. In **2 Samuel**, He is **the prophesied Son of David**
11. In **1 Kings**, He is the **One greater than Solomon**
12. In **2 Kings**, He is the **Holiest of all**
13. In **1 Chronicles,** He is the **King by birth**
14. In **2 Chronicles,** He is the **King by judgement**
15. In **Ezra,** He is the Lord of **Heaven and Earth**
16. In **Nehemiah,** He is the **great Builder**
17. In **Esther**, He is **Unseen Hand**
18. In **Job,** He is the **Living Redeemer**
19. In **Psalms,** He is the **Good Shepherd and the coming Messiah**

20. In **Proverbs,** He is **our Wisdom**
21. In **Ecclesiastes,** He is **the truth above the sun**
22. In the **Song of Solomon,** He is **the Rose of Sharon**
23. In **Isaiah,** He is **Wonderful, Counsellor, the Mighty God, the Everlasting Father**
24. In **Jeremiah,** He is the **Lord our Righteousness**
25. In **Ezekiel,** He is **the Prince who enters the Eastern Gate**
26. In **Daniel,** He is **the Ancient of Days**
27. In **Hosea,** He is the **Risen Son of God**
28. In **Joel,** He is the **One roaring out of Zion**
29. In **Amos,** He is the **One standing upon the altar.**
30. In **Obadiah,** He is the **Humbler of Edom's pride**
31. In **Jonah,** He is the **Risen Prophet.**
32. In **Micah,** He is the **Ruler of Israel**
33. In **Nahum,** He is our **Stronghold in the day of wrath**
34. In **Habakkuk,** He is the **Lord in His Holy Temple**
35. In **Zephaniah, He is the Lord in the midst**
36. In **Haggai,** He is **the desire of all nations**

37. In **Zechariah**, He is the **One wounded in the house of His friends**
38. In **Malachi**, He is the **Sun of Righteousness.**
39. In **Matthew**, He is the **King of the Jews**
40. In **Mark**, He is the **servant of the Lord**
41. In **Luke**, He is the **Son of Man**
42. In **John**, He is the **Son of God**
43. In **Acts**, He is the **Builder of the Church**
44. In **Romans**, He is the **Justifier of him who believes.**
45. In **1 Corinthians**, He is the **first-fruits from among the dead**
46. In **2 Corinthians**, He is **the unspeakable gift**
47. In **Galatians**, He is the **Seed of Abraham**
48. In **Ephesians**, He is **Head of the Church**
49. In **Philippians**, He is the **supplier of every need**.
50. In **Colossians**, He is the **preeminent One**
51. In **1 Thessalonians**, He is **the returning Lord**
52. In **2 Thessalonians**, He is **the soon coming King.**
53. In **1 Timothy**, He is **God manifest in the flesh**
54. In **2 Timothy**, He is the Lord, the **righteous judge**

55. In **Titus**, He is the **Blessed Hope**
56. In **Philemon**, He is **Saviour of Slaves**
57. In **Hebrews**, He is **the High Priest**
58. In **James**, He is the **Judge standing before the door**
59. In **1 Peter**, He is the **chief shepherd**
60. In **2 Peter**, He is the **day star arising in our heart**
61. In **1 John**, **He is our Advocate**
62. In **2 John**, He is **the confession of one who is true**
63. In **3 John**, He is **source of prosperity**
64. In **Jude**, He is **coming with ten thousands of his saints**
65. In **Revelation**, He is **King of Kings and Lord of Lords**

He is found in every corner of the scripture.

CHANGE OF BARTON

[16]Let your light so shine before men, that they may see your good works and glorify your Father in heaven. [17] "Do not think that I came to destroy the Law or the Prophets. I did not come to destroy but to fulfil. [18]For assuredly, I say to you, till heaven and earth pass away, one jot or one tittle

will by no means pass from the law till all is fulfilled. **Matthew 5:16-17**

*"Then He said to them, "These are the words which I spoke to you while I was still with you, that all things must be fulfilled which were written in the **Law** of Moses and the **Prophets** and the Psalms concerning Me."* **Luke 24:44**

After his temptations in the wilderness and at the start of His ministry Jesus declared:

"From that time Jesus began to preach and to say, "Repent, for the kingdom of heaven is at hand." **Matthew 4:17**

"but He said to them, "I must preach the kingdom of God to the other cities also, because for <u>this purpose I have been sent</u>." **Luke 4:43**

And to finally confirm this, Jesus took three of his disciples to witness a handover ceremony:

Matthew 17
¹ *Now after six days Jesus took Peter, James, and John his brother, led them up on a high mountain by themselves;* ²*and He was transfigured before them. His face shone like the*

sun, and His clothes became as white as the light. **³And behold, Moses and Elijah appeared to them, talking with Him.** ⁴Then Peter answered and said to Jesus, "Lord, it is good for us to be here; if You wish, let us[ ] make here three tabernacles: one for You, one for Moses, and one for Elijah."

⁵**While he was still speaking,** (God shut him and his religious spirit up) behold, a bright cloud overshadowed them; and suddenly a voice came out of the cloud, saying, "This is My beloved Son, in whom I am well pleased. Hear Him!" ⁶And when the disciples heard it, they fell on their faces and were greatly afraid. ⁷But Jesus came and touched them and said, "Arise, and do not be afraid." ⁸**When they had lifted up their eyes, they saw no one but Jesus only.** (the Law and the prophet were gone). ⁹Now as they came down from the mountain, Jesus commanded them, saying, "Tell the vision to no one until the Son of Man is risen from the dead." ¹⁰And His disciples asked Him, saying, "Why then do the scribes say that Elijah must come first?"

¹¹Jesus answered and said to them, "Indeed, Elijah is coming first[ ] and will restore all things. ¹²But I say to you that Elijah has come already, and they did not know him but did to him whatever they wished. Likewise the Son of Man is also about to suffer at their hands." ¹³Then the disciples

understood that <u>He spoke to them of John the Baptist.</u> (See also Mal. 4:1-5 ; Luke 1:11-17)

KEY POINTS TO NOTE:

1. This meeting on the mountain was not all about transfiguration; it was also about Transferring.
2. Jesus as it were "picked up the Barton" from Moses (the Law) and Elijah (The Prophets). **Luke 16 [NLT]** - *[16]"Until John the Baptist began to preach, the laws of Moses and the messages of the prophets were your guides. <u>But now the Good News of the Kingdom of God is preached,</u>*
3. The conversation on the mount between Moses, Elijah and Jesus was about the closure of an assignment and the start of a new one, (the gospel of the kingdom).
4. Peter had a religious spirit, which afflicts many churches today. He wanted to build monuments to the dead. Many of us are busy building monuments to for the dead. God is not in it.
5. After the Voice came from heaven that confirmed the transfer that just took place;

when the disciples looked, it was only Jesus that remained. Now the Law and the Prophets have had their day. Jesus is the only one we must now preach.

6. Before John the Baptist all that could be preached was the Law and the Prophets, but when Jesus came the prophets was fulfilled and the law was fulfilled under a new grace of God. **John 1:45-** *Philip found Nathanael and said to him, "We have found Him of whom Moses in the **law**, and also the **prophets**, wrote--Jesus of Nazareth, the son of Joseph."* **Romans 3:21-** *But now the righteousness of God apart from the **law** is revealed, being witnessed by the **Law** and the **Prophets**.*

We are henceforth mandated to preach only the **gospel of the Kingdom** and reign on earth like Kings exercising Authority and Dominion over all things. Jesus then conferred on us the kingship of this Kingdom:

Daniel 7:18 - [18] *But the saints of the Most High will receive the kingdom and will possess it forever-yes, for ever and ever.'*

Luke 22:29 - ²⁹And _I bestow upon you a kingdom_, just as My Father bestowed one upon Me, ³⁰that you may eat and drink at My table in My kingdom, and sit on thrones judging the twelve tribes of Israel."

Luke 12:32- ³²"Do not fear, little flock, for it is your Father's good pleasure _to give you the kingdom_.

A Kingdom is a Governing Authority that influences its territories. If we understand what the kingdom is, we will then be able to understand who the Kings of the kingdom should be and the Keys with which to enter the Kingdom.

Isaiah 9:6-7 - For unto us a Child is born, Unto us a Son is given; And _the government will be upon His shoulder_. And His name will be called Wonderful, Counsellor, Mighty God, Everlasting Father, Prince of Peace. Of the _increase of His government_ and peace There will be no end, Upon the **throne of David** and over _His kingdom_, To order it and establish it with judgment and justice From that time forward, even forever. The zeal of the Lord of hosts will perform this.

Kingdom Dominion is about CITIZENSHIP & GOVERNANCE.

Kingdom of Heaven is A PLACE (of which we can experience from the earth); while the **Kingdom of God is** GOD'S WAY OF DOING THINGS. HIS VALUES, HIS PRINCIPLES --- THEREFORE HIS WORD. The Word of God is still the final authority in all things.

Matthew 4 - *[17]From that time Jesus began to preach and to say, "Repent, for the <u>kingdom of heaven</u> is at hand."*

Luke 4 - *[43]but He said to them, "I must preach the <u>kingdom of God</u> to the other cities also, because for <u>this purpose I have been sent</u>."*

So Jesus came to preach the <u>Kingdom of God</u> so that we can be ready to receive and enter the <u>Kingdom of Heaven.</u> You have **no business with the <u>kingdom of heaven</u> if you do not live your life in the <u>kingdom of God.</u>**

For example America is a place and also a value system. You cannot live in America (the place) if you do not believe in the America (the value system and way of life). How can people live in heaven when they do not know God's ways of doing things? The Kingdom of God is revealed in the WORD of God. Obeying the word of God establishes the Kingdom of God in you. OBEDIENCE TO THE WORD OF GOD IS THE KEY TO RULERSHIP IN GOD'S KINGDOM on Earth.

Recognising the voice of the Holy Spirit is the greatest asset to any believer's destiny.

OUR INSTRUMENTS OF RULERSHIP & DOMINION AS A RESULT OF DIVINE GUIDANCE

Psalm 23:1-6 -[1] *The LORD is my shepherd; I shall not want.* [2]*He makes me to lie down in green pastures; He leads me beside the still waters.* [3]*He restores my soul; He leads me in the paths of righteousness For His name's sake.* [4]*Yea, though I walk through the valley of the shadow of death, I will fear no evil; For You are with me; Your rod and Your staff, they comfort me.* [5]*You prepare a table before me in the presence of my enemies; You anoint my head with oil; My cup runs over.* [6]*Surely goodness and mercy shall follow* *me All the days of my life; And I will dwell in the house of the LORD Forever.*

1. **Divine Guidance commands DIVNE PROVISION. – Verse 1.** *Like Elijah. 1Kings 17*

2. **Divine Guidance commands DIVINE REST. Vs 2-3.** *You will cease struggling, Heb. 4:1-11.* **REST is an expression of Dominion.**

3. **Divine Guidance commands DIVINE CONFIDENCE. Vs 4A.** *Cast not away your confidence. Isa. 30:15*

4. **Divine Guidance commands DIVINE CONQUEST. Vs 4B-5A.** *God shows you off. Conquest is where your mere presence disarms the enemy.*

5. **Divine Guidance commands DIVINE EMPOWERMENT. Vs 5B.** *Oil represents the anointing.*

6. **Divine Guidance commands DIVINE FAVOUR. Vs 6A.**

7. Divine Guidance commands DIVINE SECURITY. Vs 6B

These are the seven instruments of Dominion available to all the children of God. These seven instruments should be present in your life as you interact with heaven and hear His voice and directives. Behind every supernatural exploit is divine guidance. The reality of God's power is manifested through obedience to Divine Direction obtained by interacting with heaven from the earth. REMEMBER: It was God that told Abraham to move. It was God that told Isaac not to go to Egypt, but to Gera. *Our provision is at the place of obedience to God's voice.*

Isaiah 42:18-24 - *[18]"Oh, how deaf and blind you are toward me! Why won't you listen? Why do you refuse to see? [19]Who in all the world is as blind as my own people, my servant? Who is as deaf as my messengers? Who is as blind as my chosen people, the servant of the LORD? [20]You see and understand what is right but refuse to act on it. You hear, but you don't really listen." [21]The LORD has magnified his law and made it truly glorious. Through it he had planned to show the world that he is righteous. [22]But what a sight his people are, for they have been robbed,* *enslaved, imprisoned, and trapped. They are fair game for all and have no one to protect them. 23Will not even one of you apply these lessons from the past and see the ruin that awaits you? 24Who allowed Israel to be robbed and hurt? Was it not the LORD? It was the LORD whom we sinned against, for the people would not go where he sent them, nor would they obey his law.*

When a Christian is spiritually deaf or blind; his destiny is in Prison. You were born for dominion. You are the light of the world. Obedience to God's word and voice brings dominion. As you interact between heaven and earth; you will begin to be guided by the voice of the spirit to exercise dominion in the kingdom of God on earth. Step out and become all that God wants you to be. God bless you.

Sons of God Manifesting Dominion

18 For I consider that the sufferings of this present time are not worthy to be compared with the glory which shall be revealed in us. 19 For the earnest expectation of the creation eagerly waits for the revealing of the sons of God. 20 For the creation was subjected to futility, not willingly, but because of Him who subjected it in hope; 21 because the creation itself also will be delivered from the bondage of corruption into the glorious liberty of the children of God. 22 For we know that the whole creation groans and labours with birth pangs together until now. Romans 8:18-22

"...Yet what we suffer now is nothing compared to the glory He will reveal to us later. For all creation is WAITING EAGERLY for that future day when GOD WILL REVEAL WHO HIS CHILDREN REALLY ARE... (NLV).

"...For I reckon that the sufferings of this present time are not worthy to be compared to THE GLORY which shall be revealed IN us...For the earnest expectation of the creature waiteth for the manifestation of the sons of God" (Romans 8:18, 19 KJV).

As we understand dominion better, through interactions between heaven and earth, we are able to shine as the Sons of God. The truth is once the coming to manifestation of the sons is revealed, something happens to the bondage of corruption to which this earth belongs. Hence, the reason why the true sons must manifest in order to bring an end to corruption is because corruption was brought to the earth through the sons of God. There was no corruption on the earth until Adam rebelled against God and the whole creation consequently rebelled against Adam. Thus, the ability to replenish and subdue the earth was lost in the rebellion. Nonetheless, if you desire to operate in peace, harmony, and have all things respond to you as they should, then this is a timely book you can't afford to ignore.

"...Jesus...asked His disciples, saying, "Who do men say that I, the Son of Man, am?" So they said, "Some say John the Baptist, some Elijah, and others Jeremiah or one of the prophets." He said to them, "But who do you say that I am?" Simon Peter answered and said, "You are the Christ, the Son of the living God." Jesus answered and said to him, "Blessed are you, Simon Bar-Jonah, for FLESH AND BLOOD HAS NOT REVEALED THIS TO YOU, BUT MY FATHER WHO IS IN HEAVEN"– Matthew 16:13-17

There is a revelation of the Spirit; there is a also revelation of the flesh. Just as the Spirit of God reveals knowledge of the plan and purpose of God for His church and entire humanity at large to those who are connected to Him, in like manner, there are revelations that come from flesh and blood. If flesh and blood does not reveal knowledge, Jesus would not have affirmed the source of the revelation of Himself which Peter received from the Father.

On the contrary, flesh and blood revelations are cerebral calculation, logic, human permutations, strong analytical and persuasive word that beguiles people to believe lying wonders; flesh and blood revelation is nothing but divination. The Sadducees, Pharisees, and the religious gurus of Jesus' days; had nothing but flesh and blood revelation of who Jesus was. But as for those who would manifest the days of heaven on earth, their manifestation would depend on the true revelation of who Jesus Christ really is. Thus you cannot manifest Jesus except He is revealed in and through you.

Although the Scriptures make it plain that flesh and blood cannot inherit the kingdom of God, there is another flesh and blood that is prepared by God for the purpose of expressing His fullness through human vessels. The Word that became flesh is called another flesh (Jesus Christ). – John 1:1, 14. And just as we have borne the image of the earthly man (first Adam) so we

Epilogue

will bear the image of the heavenly man (the last Adam—Jesus Christ). –1 Corinthians 15:49, 45. Those that would posses another flesh in order to manifest the image of the heavenly Man are the ones that are not born after the will of flesh and blood, nor of the will of man, but after the will of God. The Son of God, Jesus Christ, went through process so that He could become the Son of Man.

In like manner, He would take us through process so that we also can become the true sons of God that would manifest Christ on earth. Although Peter received the true revelation of who Jesus is, he was forbidden from preaching it because he had not gone through the process whereby the word would become flesh in him. In other words, until the word becomes flesh in you, you cannot preach Him effectively. – John 1:12, 13; Romans 8:14; 2 Peter 1:16-19; Luke 2:21; Isaiah 9:6; Matthew 3:13-17.

The flesh and blood that would inherit the kingdom of God are those that have the life of Christ in them. When Jesus said except we eat His flesh and drink His blood we have no life in us, He simply means only those who feed on His truth and consume His grace, and feed on His life would manifest Him and represent His purpose and interest on planet earth. Thus we eat His flesh and drink His blood. The Bible says the life of an animal is in the blood, therefore only those who feed on His life are the true sons of God that would manifest and represent Him and do His will in all ramifications. Therefore as we feed on His flesh and drink His blood, we possess eternal life. We have another life that nothing in this world can equal. – John 6:50-58; 1 Corinthians 15:50; 10:16, 17; 11:25, 26; John 17:1-3.

Note: whatever revelation of God you might have received does not immediately translate into manifestation until it is processed **in** and **through** you. Unfortunately, many people want revelation but they are not ready to pay the price that would bring the revelation into manifestation. *Going through the process of manifestation is what would hinder many from coming into manifestation.* God has to prepare you for what He has prepared for you—He has to make you ready! Because *It takes process for revelation to produce manifestation in you.*

Everyone that would represent God and operate by the standard of heaven in every facet of human endeavour would go through conception and gestation period before manifestation can take place. In other words, the revelation you conceived must go through gestation in you before you can manifest it. *The ultimate next level is that the life of Jesus may be manifested in our mortal flesh.* Next level has nothing to do with temporary or material things; they are things of eternal worth! If all we want to do is show off that our God is mighty by material things, then, we have short-changed our generation. – Matthew 16:21, 22; 2 Corinthians 4:11.

Those that would not see death until they see the Son of Man coming in His Kingdom are those that would allow God to take them through the process of birthing Christ in their heart, and they would not jump the gun until the Master makes them ready for His use. But it is unfortunate that the Church has limited the manifestation of the kingdom of God to an unprecedented event that would take place in the future. **Brethren, it is high time we understood that**

the manifestation of the kingdom through tested and seasoned vessels is now!

Christ is not coming for a weak Church, but rather for a strong and vibrant Church. He must work His works in you before He can do His works through you. - Galatians 1:10- 19; 2:1, 2; Matthew 16:21-28; Luke 9:18-26; Matthew 17:1-13. Furthermore, in the entire Scriptures, the word manifestation occurs only three times — the manifestation of the Spirit — 1 Corinthians 12:7; the manifestation of truth — 2 Corinthians 4: 2, and the manifestation of the sons of God — Romans 8: 19. In other words, the sons of God cannot come into manifestation except the manifestation of truth and the Spirit merge in them. The word did not become flesh until Mary believed the revelation that was told her before the Holy Spirit came upon her. That is, it is the manifestation of the truth and of the Spirit merging in a child of God, which becomes a reality that he has embraced that causes his manifestation.

The manifestation of the sons (believers) of God is the manifestation of the Son (Jesus Christ) of God. It is Christ manifesting Himself through the believers.

Epilogue

Thus they become godly people. A godly man is not one who goes to Church, but one who has opened himself to God so that God can manifest Himself through that individual. —Titus 1:1-3; John 1:1-14; 1Timothy 3:16.

No one can preach or represent Christ effectively unless Christ reveals Himself in the life of that individual. In other words, you cannot manifest Christ except the word is manifested *in* you, *through* you, and *to* you. The word of God must become the final authority in your life without any reserve, regard or respect for human opinion and the philosophy of man.

The highest manifestation of God is His word.

Jesus is the light, life, and love. Therefore, the manifestation of light, life, and love must take their full cause in your life before you can manifest Him. The manifestation of the true sons of God is contingent upon whether the Spirit and the truth is manifesting in them and through them. Until His word and light produce light in you, you cannot manifest Him. You cannot manifest God until you become a personification of His word, light, life, and His love. –1 John 1:5; 2:8; 1:1-7; 4:7-21. The manifestation of the Word of God in us as Children of God will involve the ability to create circumstances by our words. God brought the earth into existence by His word.

We also can bring the Kingdom of God into existence by our authoritative declaration of the word of God? So the Word, spoken in authority is a key instrument of our dominion living. Never forget that. Our confession must reflect our authority in heaven and not our temporal circumstances here on earth. Like the centurion said to Jesus, all you have to do is speak the word and change will be effected. So, go out today and begin to dominate the earth through your words as God perfects His work in you. You are blessed and highly favoured. Shalom.

In the sequel to this book, we will be looking at Marketplace Dominion. How believers can dominate the marketplace on their journey to the Wealthy Place. With the foundation laid in this book; you are now ready to engage with the marketplace and invade it with righteousness; knowing that the weapons of our warfare are not canal, but mighty through God. The Marketplace is the final frontier....and we are invading it with Righteousness. Get ready for the final push. Jesus is Lord.

Other Books by Pastor Charles Omole

1. **Church, Its time to Fly** -- *Learning to fly on Eagles Wing.*

2. **How to Avoid Getting Hurt in Church** -- *13 Steps that will protect you and help create an atmosphere for breakthroughs.*

3. **Must I go to Church** -- *8 Reasons why you must attend Church.*

4. **Freedom from Condemnation** -- *Breaking free from the burden and weight of sin.*

5. **I cannot serve a big God and remain small**

6. **How to start your own business**

7. **How to Make Godly Decisions**

8. **How to avoid financial collapse**

9. **Let Brotherly love continue:** *An insight into love and companionship.*

10. **Breaking out of the debt trap**

11. **Common Causes of Unanswered Prayer.**

12. **How to Argue with God and Win** -- *Biblical strategies on getting God's attention for all your circumstances all of the time*

13. **Avoiding Power Failure** -- *How to generate spiritual power for daily success and victorious living.*

14. **How long should I continue to pray when I don't see an answer?**

15. **SUCCESS KILLERS:** *Seven Habits of Highly Ineffective Christians.*

16. **The Financial Resource Handbook** – UK Edition

17. **Divine Strategies for uncommon breakthroughs:** *Living in the Reality of the Supernatural:*

18. **Keys to Divine Success**

19. **Wrong Thoughts, Wrong Emotion and Wrong Living**

20. **Secrets of Biblical Wealth Transfer**

21. **Journey to Fulfilment** – *From Singleness, to Marriage and Raising Children; How to make yours a Journey into fulfilment.*

22. **Prosperity Unleashed** – *A Definitive Guide to Biblical Economics*

23. **No More Debt** – *Volume 1*

24. **Understanding Dominion**

For more information about our ministry, world outreaches and a free catalogue of our media and study materials, please write to:

Winning Faith Outreach Ministries

151 Mackenzie Road
London. N7 8NF
UNITED KINGDOM
www.charlesomole.org
info@charlesomole.org

Another Best-seller from Pastor Charles Omole

Another Best-seller from Pastor Charles Omole

Other Books

Another Best-seller from Pastor Charles Omole

Understanding Dominion

Another Best-seller from Pastor Charles Omole

Another Best-seller from Pastor Charles Omole

Another Best-seller from Pastor Charles Omole

www.ingramcontent.com/pod-product-compliance
Lightning Source LLC
Chambersburg PA
CBHW020851090426
42736CB00008B/328